signature

HUNTER DUKES

T0024289

BLOOMSBURY ACADEMIC
NEW YORK • LONDON • OXFORD • NEW DELHI • SYDNEY

BLOOMSBURY ACADEMIC
Bloomsbury Publishing Inc
1385 Broadway, New York, NY 10018, USA
50 Bedford Square, London, WC1B 3DP, UK

BLOOMSBURY, BLOOMSBURY ACADEMIC and the Diana logo
are trademarks of Bloomsbury Publishing Plc

First published in the United States of America 2020

Cover design: Alice Marwick

Library of Congress Cataloging-in-Publication Data
Names: Dukes, Hunter, author.
Title: Signature / Hunter Dukes.
Description: New York: Bloomsbury Academic, 2020. | Series: Object lessons |
Includes bibliographical references and index. | Summary: "30,000-year-old handprints,
animal scent, celebrity autographs, air trapped in Antarctic ice, and graffiti tags are
all signatures-a seldom explored form of marking that reveals something
fundamental about what it means to have a body"– Provided by publisher.
Identifiers: LCCN 2020029920 (print) | LCCN 2020029921 (ebook) |
ISBN 9781501353345 (paperback) | ISBN 9781501353338 (epub) |
ISBN 9781501353314 (pdf)
Subjects: LCSH: Signatures (Writing) | Autographs.
Classification: LCC Z41 .D85 2020 (print) | LCC Z41 (ebook) | DDC 929.8/8–dc23
LC record available at https://lccn.loc.gov/2020029920
LC ebook record available at https://lccn.loc.gov/2020029921

ISBN: PB: 978-1-5013-5334-5
ePDF: 978-1-5013-5331-4
eBook: 978-1-5013-5333-8

Series: Object Lessons

Typeset by Deanta Global Publishing Services, Chennai, India
Printed and bound in the United States of America

To find out more about our authors and books visit www.bloomsbury.com
and sign up for our newsletters.

"The Object Lessons series achieves something very close to magic: the books take ordinary—even banal—objects and animate them with a rich history of invention, political struggle, science, and popular mythology. Filled with fascinating details and conveyed in sharp, accessible prose, the books make the everyday world come to life. Be warned: once you've read a few of these, you'll start walking around your house, picking up random objects, and musing aloud: 'I wonder what the story is behind this thing?'"

Steven Johnson, author of *Where Good Ideas Come From* and *How We Got to Now*

"Object Lessons describe themselves as 'short, beautiful books,' and to that, I'll say, amen. . . . If you read enough Object Lessons books, you'll fill your head with plenty of trivia to amaze and annoy your friends and loved ones—caution recommended on pontificating on the objects surrounding you. More importantly, though . . . they inspire us to take a second look at parts of the everyday that we've taken for granted. These are not so much lessons about the objects themselves, but opportunities for self-reflection and storytelling. They remind us that we are surrounded by a wondrous world, as long as we care to look."

John Warner, *The Chicago Tribune*

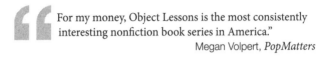 For my money, Object Lessons is the most consistently
interesting nonfiction book series in America."
Megan Volpert, *PopMatters*

Besides being beautiful little hand-sized objects
themselves, showcasing exceptional writing, the
wonder of these books is that they exist at all . . .
Uniformly excellent, engaging, thought-provoking, and
informative."
Jennifer Bort Yacovissi, *Washington Independent
Review of Books*

. . . edifying and entertaining . . . perfect for slipping in a
pocket and pulling out when life is on hold."
Sarah Murdoch, *Toronto Star*

[W]itty, thought-provoking, and poetic . . . These little
books are a page-flipper's dream."
John Timpane, *The Philadelphia Inquirer*

Though short, at roughly 25,000 words apiece, these
books are anything but slight."
Marina Benjamin, *New Statesman*

The joy of the series, of reading *Remote Control*, *Golf Ball*, *Driver's License*, *Drone*, *Silence*, *Glass*, *Refrigerator*, *Hotel*, and *Waste* . . . in quick succession, lies in encountering the various turns through which each of their authors has been put by his or her object. . . . The object predominates, sits squarely center stage, directs the action. The object decides the genre, the chronology, and the limits of the study. Accordingly, the author has to take her cue from the *thing* she chose or that chose her. The result is a wonderfully uneven series of books, each one a *thing* unto itself."

Julian Yates, *Los Angeles Review of Books*

The Object Lessons series has a beautifully simple premise. Each book or essay centers on a specific object. This can be mundane or unexpected, humorous or politically timely. Whatever the subject, these descriptions reveal the rich worlds hidden under the surface of things."

Christine Ro, *Book Riot*

. . . a sensibility somewhere between Roland Barthes and Wes Anderson."

Simon Reynolds, author of *Retromania: Pop Culture's Addiction to Its Own Past*

OBJECTLESSONS

A book series about the hidden lives of ordinary things.

Series Editors:

Ian Bogost and Christopher Schaberg

Advisory Board:

Sara Ahmed, Jane Bennett, Jeffrey Jerome Cohen, Johanna
Drucker, Raiford Guins, Graham Harman, renée hoogland,
Pam Houston, Eileen Joy, Douglas Kahn, Daniel Miller,
Esther Milne, Timothy Morton, Kathleen Stewart, Nigel
Thrift, Rob Walker, Michele White

In association with

Georgia Tech ⚊ Center for Media Studies

BOOKS IN THE SERIES

For my parents, Sally and Timothy Dukes,
whose signatures I carry.

. . . the handprint which signs the cave-painting, the writing on the wall at Belshazzar's feast, the miraculous images deposited on the handkerchief of Veronica, or the Shroud of Turin . . . the fingerprint of the burglar, the silhouettes seared upon the wall at Hiroshima, and even the signature coiled in my DNA . . .
—STEVEN CONNOR, *THE BOOK OF SKIN*

CONTENTS

1 THE DOTTED LINE

We rarely perceive our own signatures. When did you last study yours? They are supposed to be habitual, automatic—lines that disappear into the background of life. But if we injure our writing hand, or sign with an unruly instrument, the autograph may leap back into presence, become strange once again. Something like this happened to me years ago, in an unlikely place: not at the UK university where I had enrolled for graduate school, but in my local pub.

Paying with an American credit card can be a puzzling ritual when abroad. While our Visas and Mastercards are now equipped with microchips, they often lack the PIN (Personal Identification Number) codes that govern European commerce; instead, a signature is required. It has been an empty formality in the United States for some time: a dash under a waiter's blind eyes. Credit card companies finally recognized this in 2018, allowing merchants to go "signature free" for most transactions. But several financial services continue to require signatures for payments over a certain threshold.[1]

British publicans have been known to respect the signature. The card reader's demanding chirp, its prompt for an autograph, occasionally triggers a decorous procedure, both charming and mad: handwriting analysis between packets of crisps. It was my first year in England. I spoke the language and I didn't. *Keen, pitch, sarnie, toff, twee, bap, batty, bop,* what? Trying to make these funny words my own, I adopted a *woeful* mid-Atlantic accent—think less FDR, more Bermuda Triangle—and laid it on thicker than treacle. In retrospect, I sounded like the lock-jawed lovechild of William F. Buckley and Lauren Bacall, with a kazoo for a larynx, whose husky pronunciation of "whine" and "wheel" positively whistled. I am still embarrassed by the brio (and of the frequency with which I used words like *brio*), by the indulgences of language, the affected signature of my adolescent self.

We were in a gallant tavern. Equal parts town and gown, it lacked only a carpet stained with ambiguous fluids (the signature fug of a good boozer, or so someone said). Autumn's seasonal depression had begun to swamp the country: a bland and general sogginess, like the pub's battered cod. Colleagues explained that *my round* had come. I elbowed toward the barman, bald with spectacles, his fingers thicker than the brushed steel jigger they held. *All right?* he asked. *Yeah, I'm doing pretty well, thanks, and how are you?* He blinked. (If you don't know: the proper response to *all right?* is to ask it right back—the "I'm rubber, you're glue" mode of hailing.) My order proceeded anyway, to something called *real ale*. I was in England, Albion, Blighty, baby. Authenticity or bust.

The barman grabbed a pendant light, swung it over the signed receipt. Then he asked to see my card.

"Sorry, isn't you."
"Sorry?"
"Isn't your signature, that."
"Whose is it?"
"Looks like another gent's."
"Another gent's?"
[*blink*]
"You mean, like, someone you know?"
"You know what?"
"What?"
"Right."

Exhibit one: a shaky scrawl, still wet around its edges. Exhibit two: my credit card's looping signature, confidently inscribed several years earlier, now rubbed out. I wanted to say bollocks to his assessment or practice some regional, East Anglian insults, recently acquired. But the pint-puller was right. These signatures shared little resemblance, except for a name, scarcely discernible in each.

And why should they have? If an autograph is the legal shorthand of an individual's agency and consent, the stamp of his presence at a specific time and place, would it not be a dynamic thing? I had changed in the intervening years; my signature had changed too, it seemed. Standing at that sticky counter I was thrown into a momentary crisis, the acute experience of derealization.

"Put a man on the moon," growled the beast of bitter, "think they could figure out chip and PIN!" Fair shout. Unpersuaded by a California driver's license, he reversed the card charges; we settled up with cash. The pints were mine, but the thought that I could be dispossessed of my signature, suddenly, by a stranger, left me shaken, stirred. Even my autograph knew I was faking it.

* * *

What are signatures? They are seismographs of personality. A mountainous horizon drawn by Etch A Sketch, with rolling peaks and troughs. Or, if slant and dense, the synthesizer's sawtooth wave, each letter breaking into the next. When scribbled in haste on a tablet's screen, names seem closer to cardiograms than autographs: the trace of a rhythmic life. Signatures are transient, too—the ink fades while you look away, like contrails dissolving into blue.

We grant them more authority than other forms of writing. The name gains fortitude from the shape of its letters, their unique, graphological profile. Your autograph is a paradox: both a failed improvisation and an unfaithful copy. Discussing the contradiction of signatures, Mario Carpo distinguishes between sameness and similarity.[2] Every signature is a repetition, but with difference; Sonja Neef calls this property *iterable uniqueness*.[3] The exact same signature, signed twice, would be a forgery. While any shape signed by your hand should be, de facto, a working signature, authentication relies upon another party: a person, institution, or object that confirms its past iterations.

Think about chicken scratch, the power it commands! A signed confession binds you to a crime and its requisite punishment; if a petition receives enough signatures, it can change the course of history; with a good forgery, a thief comes one step closer to stealing an identity, becoming *you* before the law. "Great is the hand that holds dominion over / Man by a scribbled name," wrote Dylan Thomas.[4] Are you surprised, then, that *making a deal with the devil* revolves around an autograph? Faust signed his agreement with Mephistopheles in blood.

Why are signatures vulnerable to interference? Because at the moment of creation they take on a life of their own. When someone signs their name, argues David Wills *pace* Jacques Derrida, they have potentially created "something that will function beyond the term of one's mortal existence."[5] Or, to quote Josh Lauer: "every signature is a memorial."[6] They are effective techniques for leaving a trace on the planet. We do not bring them with us when we go. Signatures stay on as relics, staving off oblivion, fossilized versions of our former selves.

But even our own signatures can turn against us, in pubs and elsewhere. Charles Lamb recounts an unnerving scene during his 1823 essay, "Oxford in the Vacation," when discussing George Dyer, *the most absent of men*. Dyer drops in on a friend and finding them away, signs the guestbook kept for missed encounters. Hours later, he returns; again he enquires; and again he asks to leave his name: "the book is brought, and in the line just above that in which he is about to print his second name (his re-script)—his first name (scarce dry) looks out upon him like another Sosia, or as if a man should suddenly encounter his own duplicate!"[7] The reference is to Plautus's *Amphitryon* in which the god Mercury disguises himself as Sosia, the slave of a Theban general, and proceeds to attack his likeness. Our signatures create replica selves, which are startling to confront. If they differ, we are disowned; when they cohere, we can feel usurped. In the play, Sosia is terrified. Wouldn't you be?

Signatures teach us a lesson about classification. They are mercurial constellations, lines drawn between the stars of an overcast sky. A name is not necessarily a signature; a signature does not need to be a name. Signatures are made through addition or subtraction, impasto and incision. Some are carved or chiseled, achieving depth, while others glide from fountain pens across a surface. (Vilém Flusser calls the former *inschrift*, the latter *aufschrift*: *in*scription vs. *on*scription.)[8] Signatures can be like birthmarks, without an alphabet, bound to the body. I am more interested in the marks birthed by a body as it moves through the world: prints, tracks, writing.

While *autograph* indicates something alphabetic, I define *signature* broadly in this book as any material trace that leads back to a body, specific or abstract, human, geologic, animal, digital, genomic, or atmospheric, in the case of *climate signatures*. For a signature to be recognized as such requires a successful instance of communication. A "unique mark" only exists within a collective understanding and regulation of those terms. Seals, autographs, and sweat patterns—secreted and impressed by the whorls on a person's fingertips—are sites of consensus: they delimit the signifying element, an iterative form.

To perceive a signature involves the capacity for recognition, something determined by the sensorium itself, its physiological and cultural limitations. Dogs can discern their own scent, but not their reflection in a mirror; fire hydrants are laden with olfactory marks that, for most of us, signify nothing. Faces are unique and recognizable because humans see them in a certain way. They would be meaningless craters of flesh should prosopagnosia ("face blindness") become a widespread condition. (Media scholars like Anna Munster would add that *faciality* is itself a "frozen" signatory structure, which solidified at a certain point in history.)[9]

Where the senses fail and the body fails to impress, others forms of signature are supplemented by technologies of preservation. Our faces do not naturally leave marks in the world (when they do, it is a miracle, like the Veil of Veronica or the Shroud of Turin). But death masks detach a facial signature from its body; photographs too. We are surprisingly good at extrapolating age, sex, mood, and other characteristics from vocal cues, but could not imprint our voices in the world until the invention of phonography.

Before "signature" signaled a squiggle, it captured a sense of *impression*. As late as the third century, Roman cursive was "too undeveloped for signatures written in it to be recognized."[10] The etymology of signature remembers an earlier technology: signums created by the authoritative impressions of a seal's matrix. In antiquity, signets featured personal silhouettes, animals, or alphabetic letters. To further personalize the waxen seal, some documents were then inscribed by a handwritten signature: "a way of putting yourself in or on a document that grew naturally out of the practice of sealing itself."[11]

Elizabeth Meyer's idea of *putting yourself* into a signature points toward the strange sense of *presence* facilitated by autographs. In the Roman Empire, they were not always names, but could be formed from entire, identifying sentences known as *subscriptio*. After the fall of Rome, Merovingian kings and noblemen used elaborate monograms to sign charters, while certain byzantine signatures, *christograms* and *cruciforms*, spliced an individual's initials *into* a Christian invocation. During seances in the nineteenth century, mediums confirmed the authenticity of spirits through automatic writing. Often the content of these messages carried less personal character than the spirit's transmitted autograph—faithful to the signatures he or she signed while alive—communicated through the medium's hand.

Signatures evolve alongside media, inscriptive technologies, and belief systems. They can be invented—in the case of *electronic signatures*—or discovered via new means of perception (*epigenetic signatures* emerged from scientific advancements in genomic sequencing and assay sensitivity). Signing is a cultural technique that marks where symbolic operations meet the material world. This is why two signatures that look nothing alike can function in similar ways. Why humans, other animals, and geologic bodies appear to partake in analogous behavior.

And autographs do things other than verify: these lines can be compelled, for profit, from an ambivalent hand ("Only one thing counts in this life," chants Alec Baldwin in *Glengarry Glen Ross*, "get them to sign on the line which is dotted!"). Refusal prevents entrapment. When asked to officially retract a statement he had never admitted to making, Major League Baseball pitcher Dizzy Dean saw through the scheme: *I ain't signin' nuthin.* Inked on a baseball, the same mark would be worth thousands today.

A shared signature creates affinity, or milks rapport. In a codicil to his will, the philosopher David Hume bequeathed his friend John Home a bottle of port, with a promise of seventy-two more, under two conditions: that he modify his signature, signing *Hume* instead of *Home*, and drink to excess from the bottle before him. "By this Concession, he will at once terminate the only two Differences, that ever arose between us . . ."[12] Signatures succumb to peer pressure, change shape under stress.

Have you seen the 2019 movie *Hustlers*? It reverses Hume's circuit: intoxicants first, then the signature. To earn money, Jennifer Lopez and her crew remain sober, drugging a rich *mark* with a mixture of ketamine and MDMA. Once their target turns giddy from the *kitty flip*, he begins "willingly" signing colossal receipts. "After you get the signature, then you can party your asses off," J.Lo tells her associates. The film is fascinating for this reason: it would be easy enough to incapacitate the victim, steal his card, or forge a signature . . . but that rarely happens. The women want to "get" the signature, not fake it—"you were having a great time" is their defense of choice. But does that deictic *you* reference the selfsame person? Can one signature stand for both a regretful banker (the morning after) and his previous evening's addled ego, hopped up on horse meds and an empathogen?

In other words, how many versions of the self can a signature carry? Virginia Woolf might answer, all of them. In her novel *The Waves*, an act of signing coalesces a man's unstable personality. The shatters of a life are bound together in his autograph.

"I have signed my name," said Louis, "already twenty times. I, and again I, and again I. Clear, firm, unequivocal, there it stands, my name. Clear-cut and unequivocal am I too. Yet a vast inheritance of experience is packed in me . . . But now I am compact; now I am gathered together this fine morning."[13]

A "vast inheritance" of divergent experiences becomes a cohesive whole, becomes *Louis* once again. The signature beads his subsequent selves. Even when a person changes across a lifetime, the autograph's power holds. More than a verification of identity, Woolf implies that the signature is a reflexive act that creates a referential subject.

Outside of fiction, the signature is no less mending. When a schoolchild breaks a bone, her friends might sign the plaster cast, as if their names will splint the fracture. But the same kind of mark may also harm. Autographing a human body can be punitive, protective, or erotic, depending on who is signing whom. In addition to *form* and *matter*, then, we need a criterion like *performance* to account for the signature's many personalities.

The philosopher of language J. L. Austin famously classed signatures as a kind of *performative utterance*, which allows an absent "I" to "come essentially into the picture."[14] He meant that the signature proxies a speaking subject, who—with a phrase like "I consent" or "I name"—changes the constitution of social reality. Austin's wording opens up another possibility too, however: that the "I" does not fully exist (that is, come *into* the picture) without a signature. A duplicate verifies its original, makes it real; "identity can only be attested to if the sign by which it is recognized has already been copied," writes Bernard Siegert.[15] (Signatures on ancient Greek art perform their attribution, keeping alive an artist's name by speaking it back into existence: *Exekias made me well*, reads a cup in the Louvre.[16])

And just as perfume allows a person to enhance their natural scent, autographic performance invites tinkering too. "From bone to air to writing, permanence outside the subject invites greater mutability," argues Douglas Kahn.[17] The history of modern penmanship (Spencerian script, the Palmer Method) rests on a belief that graphological refinement is morally edifying.[18] Nineteenth-century copybooks, like those created by Vere Foster, taught handwriting through pedagogical platitudes.[19] Perfect your signature and it might rearrange the state of your soul, or even, its fate in the afterlife. "The man with an unintelligible signature may prosper in this world," thought Rudyard Kipling, "but he will assuredly be punished in the next."[20]

* * *

For a signature to live on, it must find surrogate housing, beyond the body from which it springs. Many are nested within immovable landscapes. I did not mean to go looking for signatures, but after seven years in England, with semiannual pilgrimages to see family in California, the occasional adventure, my marriage to a Finn, and our emigration to her country, I have roamed widely recently. And met many people, who changed how I think.

This book addresses subjects as varied as ancient handprints on cave walls, Victorian autograph hunters, the medical history of signing patients' bodies, how hip-hop lyrics converge with Renaissance poetry, legal challenges to electronic signatures, and ice cores harvested from

Greenland. In the pages ahead, you will find conversations with: an autograph collector (made famous by Zadie Smith); Finland's premier rock art photographer; a tattooist raised on the Mexican-American border, who summons creatures from her unconscious (one of which now curls around my left arm); a Cycladic poet concerned with the preservation of inscriptions and animals; and other fascinating people— some quoted, some paraphrased—whom I have had the privilege of knowing. Signatures scatter the self. The following is my attempt to pull its pieces back together.

2 S FOR SIGNATURE

Orson Welles is wearing black. With a slouch hat and billowing cape, he's dressed like a magician or a cowboy villain. Washed in the shadows of a winter afternoon, his clothes swallow the color spectrum, smother escaping light. But look at the piety in that smile. Watch his face, the way it glows against the dark—his crescent beard a silver moon on screen. This is not the Welles we know. Not Will Varner from *The Long, Hot Summer*, sallow as the Technicolor gravy on his supper, nor *Touch of Evil*'s weighty Hank Quinlan, who frowns through cigar smoke at tomorrow's hangover. Gone are the prosthetic noses of former roles; the whites of *these* eyes live up to their name. They gaze in wonder upon something out of sight.

> *The premier work of man, perhaps, in the whole Western world, and it's without a signature.*

His object of address? Chartres Cathedral. We are shown the church's portals, its gothic spires, saints and angels, the great façades. Enduring works are spiritual capsules. And, without an architect's autograph, this one feels collectively made. As long as it remains intact, says Welles, there will be life after death for those ancient worshippers, their vision enclosed in a cosmos of stone. When it finally falls (as everything must), an epoch's singular achievement will be lost to alluvium, returned to the earth and its elements. *Maybe a name doesn't matter all that much after all . . .*[1]

Did Welles have precursors? He did, indeed. "What were their names? No one knows," wrote the cricketer Cecil Headlam in 1902.[2] James Wright finds only the tags of graffiti writers in his 1970 poem, "Names Scarred at the Entrance to Chartres," which he condemns as vulgar, but news-editor Gilbert Millstein has sympathy for the vandals, whose act he understands as an encounter with infinitude: "the tourist, shaken by eternity at Chartres, cuts his initials profanely into the reredos of the cathedral."[3] We grab at the coattails of immortality, embroider our names on the enduring. Why?

How can signatures inspire both reverence and antipathy? Where does an autograph store value? Is there merit in leaving something unsigned? Unlike Sacré-Cœur in Paris ("that gloomy, ponderous erection raised by men who have written their names in red on every stone!"), Chartres is praised by novelist J.-K. Huysmans for its namelessness.[4] At what age does a profane signature become profound? And must it be a name? Dorothy Molloy uncovered a different kind of mark during her visit to Chartres: "I trace the masons' signatures / on stone."[5]

Real Fake

Chartres appears at the end of *F for Fake*, a "documentary" about artistic forgery. (The scare quotes are from Welles: when asked about the film's genre, he once replied, "not a documentary—a new kind of film").[6] The director cannot evade his own investigation. He calls himself a charlatan then vows to tell us facts. We grow suspicious of filmmaking, its immersive conventions: disbelief balloons while the take-up reel spools. If reportage holds up a mirror to nature, *F for Fake* uses funhouse glass. But any discomfort is engineered. How better to discuss forgery than to put its tricks to work?

Welles makes us distrust the documentary form, its sleights of hand, the way we might distrust the paintings of Elmyr de Hory. During his career, the Hungarian forger sold countless "fakes" to international dealers—works that some claim still hang unsuspected in galleries and museums. Filmed mainly on Ibiza during the early 1970s, *F for Fake* captures Elmyr in his environs, telling tall tales over cocktails, about adventures in Kansas City, Paris, Rio de Janeiro, Stockholm, Rome.

The facts of the forger's biography are built on apocrypha. Few ever saw him paint. He was known for his dandyisms, for speaking five languages, and driving red convertibles named after animals (mustang, stingray). In his eye, a monocle; on his wrist, a Cartier. Some thought he was an exiled aristocrat. One thing is certain: Elmyr was an extraordinary faker.

He had tried to make it as a painter, but his art was muddled with the signatures of predecessors. Critics panned his exhibition at Lilienfeld Galleries in New York for being derivative and dated.[7] In need of cash, he built a business on his shortcomings. Elmyr began to paint *new* works by Renoir, Dufy, Derain, and other moderns. These "fakes" were not simple copies, but "original" works of art, done in someone else's style, often signed with someone else's name. He would live for weeks on the profits from Picasso sketches, which took only hours to create. Museums and collectors swooned for the faker's polish, bought his Matisses without suspicion. Before long, Elmyr could open books on Impressionist art and find his own work reproduced upon the page.

Two senses of signature are present in these forgeries. First, the autograph itself, which Elmyr (or his associates) duplicated more or less seamlessly. A fake is a fake is a fake, however, with or without an inscription. The autograph becomes a metonym for another kind of signature, one dispersed throughout the painting. Writing during the Italian Renaissance, Giulio Mancini compared painterly detail to personal script, as both fend off the would-be forger: "these features in a painting are like strokes and flourishes in handwriting, which require the master's boldness and resolution."[8] A forger not only copies another person's sign, he inhabits their style, a master's signature contribution to her aesthetic tradition. (In making *F for Fake*, the director effaced his own filmic signatures. He eschewed any shots that could be regarded as *Wellesian* and reused uncredited outtakes from François Reichenbach. It is as if, in order to depict the forger, Welles had to become one.[9])

* * *

The mark of *one* can stand for *many*, in many different ways. Compare Elmyr de Hory's art to a story from the history of Pueblo ceramics, sold in global markets. While overseeing pottery revivals, a representative from the Museum of New Mexico insisted that blackware master Maria Martinez "authenticate and increase the value of her pottery by signing it—something that Pueblo potters had never done," recounts Barbara Babcock. "When the other potters in the village realized that pots with Maria's signature commanded higher prices, they asked her to sign their pots as well and she freely did so until the Santa Fe authorities realized what was happening and put an end to this semiotic riot."[10] Even after she began signing her name as "Maria," "Marie," or "Poveka," many of Martinez's creations were signed twice, signaling collaboration between potter and pot painter, the latter role often performed by Julian Martinez (Pocano), Maria's husband.

The sharing of signatures harkens back to art production in Europe before the fifteenth century, before art became distinct from craft, when—according to a now controversial argument—it was not yet the expression of an individual, autonomous personality.[11] (I do not want to imply that "tribality" equates in any way with "anonymity," however, for this remains a problem in criticism of indigenous arts.) Martinez's signature becomes less an instance of forgery, more a watermark of shared cultural inheritance, which challenges the intersection of economic forces and legal frameworks seeking to enclose intellectual property and further the fiction of a singular Artist, acting in isolation. This is more than a question of ornament: signatures can reorder community. Kenneth Dauber describes how the "creation of distinctions among potters, implied by market differentiation and the practice of signing pots, had far-reaching implications for stratification within the pueblos." He proceeds to recount how labor hierarchies arose, distinguishing "named" potters from those unrecognized by "Anglo" patrons, which changed how pueblos in Santa Clara approached agriculture, weakening "communal labor obligations" and sowing disharmony.[12]

If Martinez's mark generates wealth in a certain cultural sphere fixated on the individual, Elmyr's signature unravels a parallel cult of genius, which trades on mystification and snobbery. Good forgers make us confront how aesthetic judgements often obey market forces—the recognition of a respected signature—and not vice versa. Elmyr threatens the tenets that underwrite cultivation: surely a trained eye can spot a fake; otherwise, expertise evaporates faster than turpentine. But when the forger presented five Picassos to Paul Rosenberg, a recognized expert and international dealer of the Spanish artist's works, he bought the lot without question. (There are hundreds of similar stories.) "If my work hangs in a museum for long enough," says Elmyr, "it becomes real." For *real*, read *indistinguishable*.

We tend to lump *forgeries* in with knockoffs and schlock. They are inferiorly wrought: a counterfeit not only lacks *authenticity*, it also falls apart faster, or so say the artisans. But Elmyr was a very good artist. In 2020, Minnesota's Hillstrom Museum of Art exhibited his work, borrowed from the collection of a man named—I kid you not—Mark Forgy, Elmyr's friend and the executor of his estate. The *New York Times* said the show revealed *the artist beneath the art forger*, but that misses the point: Elmyr revealed the forger beneath other artists.[13] Think of Picasso's *Les Demoiselles d'Avignon*, which, according to Jonathan Lethem, oozes *imperial plagiarism*: the "free use" of indigenous or "primitive" artworks and styles "by more privileged (and better-paid) artists."[14] Is there a notable difference between inhabiting another painter's signature and profiting off the unattributed signatures of unnamed artists?[15]

Impersonate a signature well enough, Welles implies, and the world will forget who is who. You may forget too. Just ask the talented Tom Ripley . . . or Kees van Dongen. An art dealer once brought a canvas to the Fauvist's studio, seeking authentication. Looking at the portrait of a woman with dark eyes, van Dongen felt something thaw—into his mind poured the melt of a glaciated past. He recalled the model, their studio sessions, an unexpected tryst and its slow unfolding. The painting became the signature of a vanished world, a key to open the locked rooms of involuntary memory. In the end, he signed the canvas, verifying it as genuine. Only later did the truth come out. He had signed an Elmyr.

On the Shores of Syros

I first saw *F for Fake* on the Cycladic island of Syros, among an extended group of travelers: a few familiar, many strange. We had gathered for a film festival and the chance to revive lives calcified by work and place. In our late-night conversations over *mezedes*, taken in courtyards along the port of Ermoupolis, a sentiment began to emerge. Its formation was slow and uneven (a remark here, an anecdote there) but steadily swelled into a chorus of recognition, like the intermittent cicadas perched unseen overhead.

Welles had us talking about signatures. One stubbled man, who, among other classified tasks, managed the Twitter account of an American ambassador, said he identified with Elmyr—the way his career glorified another person's name. Dressed in linen and loafers, he gripped a sweating glass of *tsipouro* and told us about a feeling that crept by him one evening in Washington. The ambassador's assistant lived in a government apartment, which came fully furnished as a perk of the job. Even the fake fruit, carefully arranged in a bowl on his kitchen table—orbs of orange and an airbrushed apple, always on the verge of spoiling—had been issued by the Department of State.

He liked not recognizing himself in his surroundings. His home had the clean anonymity of a hotel. But sometimes, trying to pacify the mind after a rote workweek, he would imagine that the bowl had been placed there *for him*. After all, the background check was thorough. Perhaps the executive branch knew about his penchant for still life, those studio art classes in college. And, after leaving the office, when he continued to work into the dim morning hours at home, he would occasionally look up and see—reflected in the bowl's rim—a pair of eyes, illuminated by his laptop's blue screen.

On the evening in question, our dinner companion had forgotten to eat. He felt empty in his furnished apartment. Physically, yes, but in other ways too. Just as the bowl contained "fruit" instead of fruit, it was as if he too had been placed into quotation marks. Names peeled off from the things that they named, and he experienced the paranoia of replication. He wondered how many of the other government employees, living in apartments above, below, and beside his own, also had a plastic horn of plenty. Perhaps some even received bananas . . . or pears. Was there a hidden message in all of this? He ended up scrolling through Twitter, searching for some imprint that he could call his own. Sometimes the ambassador tweeted; other times he outsourced the content to his assistant. But, looking over the feed, our talesman did not remember whose posts were whose. His voice had been subsumed beneath someone else's sign.

The story's crescendo became a credence. Social media platforms create the illusion of individuality, yet celebrities, officials, and other influencers rely upon advisers and copywriters to craft their content. On Twitter, the blue checkmark signature of a verified account often indicates a community of individuals, laboring together to fashion a cohesive, singular self. But at what cost? What happens to the selves who shore others' shards? Who *selves* them?

The ambassador's assistant discussed collaboration and its discontents, but there was something else at play in Elmyr's forgeries. A parasitic impulse, a fantasy unfulfilled. I was reminded of a novel. In James Joyce's *A Portrait of the Artist as a Young Man*, the character Lynch acts on a devious impulse: he graffities the Venus of Praxiteles, a statue in Dublin's National Museum, signing his name across the goddess's rear. Disguise Lynch in an artist's smock and he looks like Elmyr, I said. When museumgoers see the Venus, they will be forced to wonder about the "Lynch" who defaced her. Did the forger not seek a similar form of redirection, albeit anonymized, by making the art world question if every new discovery was not, in fact, his? Was the Ambassador leaching something vital from his hardworking assistant, something that the word "labor" no longer encompasses?

A beat in conversation; the rush of fingernails across our tabletop; and then her dialogue began. She spoke Muscovite English from beneath an onion dome of hair. The candles lit her hand, adorned by three silver rings, which, together, formed a Greek column: base, shaft, capital. So precise were the woman's gesticulations—sometimes crow straight, sometimes meandering through choreographed movements that left trails in the air like motorways photographed at night—that she seemed able to juggle light.

It was odd that I would mention the Venus. She worked as an art appraiser; recently an experiment caught her attention. A pair of artists, known as MishMash, had melted forty kilograms of pink soap into a mold. They cast a goddess. The "Pink Venus" was installed in the toilet of a Moscow canteen, popular since Soviet times. It was an exercise in ablution: visitors rubbed the installation while washing their hands. Their palms' ridges slowly smoothed the work until it resembled a body of glass, blunted by the sea.

She thought that the installation could be read as a contest of signatures: fingerprints of a collective battling the goddess, grinding down its physical identity. The statue's shifting appearance recapitulated the evolution of sculpture toward abstraction, the artists claimed. But she was more interested in how people began to interact with the Venus. At first, reverence. But then bite marks appeared on the body, along with stains, moles, scars. Some of the gnawing, by dint of its location, became undeniably sexual. "[I]s it really possible," asked MishMash in a later statement, "that an ancient goddess, a museum sculpture can cause such a human passion?"[16]

But the student of classics has seen this before! A text by Pseudo-Lucian (*pseudo* because its author was himself a faker) tells a disconcerting story about the Venus of Praxiteles. Here, let me show you, she said, opening a PDF from the Loeb Classical Library on her phone. The appraiser scrolled rapidly, thumb-wrestling the bright surface, until she found the passage sought.

> When we could admire [the statue] no more, we noticed a mark on one thigh like a stain on a dress; the unsightliness of this was shown up by the brightness of the marble everywhere else . . .
>
> The attendant woman who was standing near us told us a strange, incredible story. For she said that a young man of a not undistinguished family—though his deed has caused him to be left nameless—who often visited the precinct, was so ill-starred as to fall in love with the goddess . . .
>
> [As] his passion grew more inflamed, every wall came to be inscribed with his messages and the bark of every tender tree told of fair Aphrodite . . . These marks of his amorous embraces were seen after day came and the goddess had that blemish to prove what she'd suffered.[17]

If we are talking about signatures, she said, then we need to consider forms of marking that are not alphabetic. Your Lynch signed his name on the Venus. But Russians are gnawing her, leaving impressions in soap. Two millennia earlier, a boy tried to satisfy his desire by inscribing temple walls and trees. When this failed, he committed an act borrowed from some kind of Pygmalion pornography, an act that stripped him of his family name. But these are all ways of signing. And not every signature is a sign of consent.

The autograph is only one way a body brands the world. What about bite marks, fingerprints, semen and saliva? It's a slippery slope from stone to flesh: lives are at stake. There is a rumor in Moscow, she said, suddenly shouting (a trait that punctuated her best stories). There is a rumor in Moscow that the canteen's butcher killed his father-in-law with a cleaver. He lost it after looking at the Venus!

I was astonished to discover, fact-checking the appraiser at a later date, that this story is true. In our correspondence, MishMash denied causality, saying the violence in no way reflected the cook's relationship to their artwork. "Allegedly, the chef (who so thoroughly and tenderly took care of the statue) killed his father-in-law and cut off his limbs. Certainly the connection between the Venus and this act of violence is a play of mind." The artists proceeded to tell me, however, about this *tenderness* in eye-catching detail: "he used some soap from her shoulder to fix a belly button, which was vandalized by the public, and finally he made it absolutely flat."

MishMash mentioned another project, where individual statues had been installed in gendered toilets. While the men's Venus was not "seriously vandalized, except for a few scratched words and hearts," they found the women's Venus "broken in pieces on the floor." They speculated about what caused "the women's anger." Was it "jealousy," the artists asked, or a violation of "cultural codes of society," the presence of a naked body in a public space?

But I wonder about this distinction between vandalization and anger. Is the act of scratching words into a body (soap or skin) really less destructive, rageful? Could the Venus have been broken, not out of anger, not out of envy, but out of sympathy or protest? Condemnation for the long, violent history of imagining female bodies as receptive surfaces for male inscriptions? Sexualized ideals of beauty? I remain haunted by these stories, their descriptive thickness. I do not yet have answers for the questions they ask.

* * *

Several nights later, we were eating octopus and discussing microplastics in the city's shipyard. The conversation had been prompted by an observation about borders: how nationalist rhetoric—the kind mongering fear about immigrants across Europe and America—exploited an older anxiety regarding the porous membranes of the biological body and the body politic. We could not have known it then, but this elision would structure how some countries handled the COVID-19 epidemic, labeling the novel coronavirus as "foreign" and neatly allying immunology and national security, as if these two defense systems were working in tandem to combat alien invaders.

Research had recently shown what has since become commonplace: synthetic compounds can be found in the bloodstreams of the Earth's most remote denizens. Our plated cephalopod was undoubtedly flush with the stuff. A filmmaker from Los Angeles began to talk about his interest in the Anthropocene, the term for an epoch of geological time in which humans are a significant force of planetary change. The previous conversation about signatures had been too focused on human forms, people and statues, he said, rolling his sleeve to reveal an orange yucca tattooed on a triceps.

We had known each other for years by then. My habit was to call him late, with a rough collection of thoughts, in no way amounting to a thesis. In return, I would receive impromptu technopagan platitudes, MP3 files of humpback whale songs, and eschatological tracts about the atom bomb. His mind was enriching, sticky. Earlier that evening, the filmmaker had announced a continued abstinence from "bovine products," believing they engendered his recurring dreams of violent death. *We extract strength from the meat that we eat . . . and memories too.* The exact mechanism eluded me, but it had something to do with the animal's stress hormones imprinting his unconscious: "beef sleep" was the term. I left that one untouched.

What interests me most about the Anthropocene is how both biological bodies and the earth cosign each other, he said. The density of pollutants in a bloodstream strongly signals the state of that body's food supply, its local waterways' purity, and the chemical composition of nearby air. Despite a lingering hallucination that we are somehow walled off from the external world, that our consciousness dwells in a corporal vacuum, this is far from the truth. We have come to accept that our physical health is subject to environmental exposure. It's not controversial to claim that cancer rates are a direct result of industrial pollution.

The idea that our sense of self, our soul, could be produced by these very same chemical *flows* is harder to swallow. And yet, this seems to be the case. Children exposed to air pollution are more likely to suffer depression later in life. Prenatal contact with the chemical BPA has been linked to the development of anxiety disorders in boys. Pesticides disrupt the way our bodies regulate hormone production, which impacts huge networks of emotion and may leave behind detectable signatures, an epigenomic record.

Not only does a body's physical health mirror the overall state of its environment, but your consciousness—the cluster of intensities that coheres into an "I"—displays the signature of a larger sphere. The phenomenologist Merleau-Ponty talked about *the chiasm*, an enfolding of the self and its world, but there's also a material link between spiritual stability and the state of the planet. One of the enduring difficulties we face when coming to terms with global heating is the complexity of analyzing a system that we have created, which, simultaneously, creates us anew.

You need not even look beyond the body to find the signature of an alien presence! We all contain at least as many cells from bacteria as the human equivalent; conversely, it is rare to find something untouched by *Homo sapiens* (said the filmmaker, waving a tentacle). Hurricanes, tornados, earthquakes—events impossible to fully model yet alone intentionally engineer—have become enmeshed with human behavior as emissions impact global weather patterns. Our collective carbon signature changes the world, and then the world changes us too.

* * *

I walked back to the hotel, through streets canopied by bougainvillea, sentried with cats. The city was built in a colorful neoclassical style, a trace of its Venetian past. And so, expecting to find blue and white buildings (the signature architecture of Cycladic isles) I was met instead with sunset tones: orange, pink, and khaki paint. Drifting off that night beneath an overhead air conditioner, mind saturated with signatures, my sleep was governed by the fan's oscillations, its mechanical, sinusoid patterns. I dreamt of kindergarten's cursive worksheets, lines of corkscrewed letters, rising and falling, repeated, across bluebook pages. How can our unique signature be born from grueling repetitions? Whose handwriting did we originally copy? And when did imitation tip over into genesis?

3 AUTOGRAPH COLLECTING

Adam Andrussier is a man out of fiction. He has made a living wheeling and dealing autographs, outbidding aficionados. While other children collected comics, he awaited celebrities—pen in hand—at the exits of concert venues. What began as a quest for "artefacts" became a profitable venture during his years at Cambridge, where he studied music. All of this gives Adam's past the air of literary character: an adolescent polymath, gaming the manuscript market between lectures and arpeggios. Adam has also been memorialized *in* fiction, however. Zadie Smith partially based Alex-Li Tandem, the protagonist of her 2002 novel *The Autograph Man*, on Andrussier.

We agree to meet on a June afternoon at his home in North London. I arrive by bus on Shoot-Up Hill (*nomen* is not *omen*, thankfully). A wrong turn leads me to Beacon Bingo, with gas torches strapped to neoclassical columns, and then, finding the right road, I pass Brent's Islamic Centre: a church retrofit with malachite domes.

It's the season when plane trees flake bark across the city, pages from a deckled book. Growths poke and wisp out of nubby pollards. If you squint, as I did, they look like pens quilled from peacock feathers held in a giant's fist. The terraced houses below are red and yellow brick. Light pools in the dimpled clay—London's take on alpenglow. These are the summer hours when even the word "scrumpy" tastes refreshing, glimpsed through the grease on an eating-house window. When signs are almost as real as the things themselves.

Years ago, I saw a faded ad for CRITERION MATCHES on the side of a nearby market. Ghost signs like these remember a different London, painted by the hands of men once called *wall dogs*. Old cities are "the quintessential place of signatures," writes the philosopher Giorgio Agamben, areas where you can still see the "signs, ciphers, or monograms that are etched onto things by time."[1] Cricklewood is such a place: a neighborhood where signatures from the past exist in visible layers, like the striation of uplifted stone.

Nowhere in London remains exempt from capital's smoothing hand. Homes sit empty amid a housing crisis in every postcode; thousands of family dwellings have been *bought to leave*, their bedrooms repurposed as deposit boxes for the rich and distant. But Cricklewood retains autonomy, its character not yet drowned out by the city's financial effusions—those glassy megaliths, the rehearsed nostalgia, its unending high streets, which slur into corporate, run-on sentences like the insane overtures of a polylingual hawker:

"PRET A MANGER GIRAFFE PIZZA EXPRESS LEON ITSU!"

I prefer it here: where graffiti bombs in bubble letters sign 1870s storefronts; where the signatures of habitants inflect local commerce, not vice versa; where restaurants making *banitsa, man'oushe, pogača, injera, pierogi, naan,* and *taftoon* share walls and customers. Zadie Smith's narrator in *On Beauty* thinks that "there is more charm in a half-mile of Cricklewood's passing human faces than in all the double-fronted Georgian houses in Primrose Hill."[2] It's a thorny sentence, equating faces and façades, making "Primrose" pull apart at its stems to evoke the prim, rosy miens of the upper class, gazing down (two-faced or double-fronted) from their elevated rise. But I didn't remember to look up. Did you?

"To Adam, from Big Daddy"

Legs crossed, Adam sits on a red sofa, wearing candy-striped socks and a dark polo shirt. There's a pot of tea, freshly brewed, between us. He asks if I am allergic to cats, gesturing toward a faintly hairy corner on the cushion where I am seated. "Not really," I say, but soon my throat begins to itch. I want to draw attention to this. We have met to discuss signatures and already my body is reacting to the trace of an absent creature, a pet that has marked its niche with scent and fur. But I am aware that, having just met Adam, I should probably pace myself. We start with origins: what ignited his lifetime interest in autographs.

"When I was on holiday with my parents in France, there was this wrestler called Big Daddy," he says without pause. "He was like the good guy and he would always have these matches against a bad guy wrestler character called Giant Haystacks. And it was kind of family fun, not full on WWF [World Wrestling Federation] style wrestling, although somewhat questionable family fun."

This is a theme that recurs during my conversation with Adam: the sense that signatures traverse innocence and experience, that an autographic impulse could tip into something both sinister and humorous. He describes his teenage membership in the Universal Autograph Collector's Club as perfectly benign, but nevertheless "the kind of thing that nowadays you might guard your children against doing, because, you know, I was a child corresponding with grown men around the world, who wanted to tell me about their collections."

When Adam speaks, he has a tendency to push his hands slowly outwards, as if sliding a rare signature toward an unseen buyer. "I was very excited to get Big Daddy's autograph," he continues, "I've still got the little piece of paper somewhere. It's funny that you remember these little details from when you are a kid. I got the hotel notepaper and he asked me to bend over so he could lean it on my back and he wrote 'To Adam, from Big Daddy.'"

I survey the room. Pots of draping palms frame the furniture, fed by rays from a bright garden. An upright piano seems frequently played, with fresh sheet music open on its stand. The wall above the keyboard displays the only four signatures that Adam keeps visible, signed photographs of jazz musicians: Billie Holiday, Fats Waller, Duke Ellington, and Bill Evans—the last autograph faded beyond appearance.

A Matisse figure captures my eye. The body's outline dances against a blue background, falling through yellow-starred space. I later discover that this is *Icarus*, collected in the collage-book *Jazz*. From my vantage, the image hangs directly behind Adam's head, peeking out when he adjusts his position. I think of Elmyr and his fake Matisses, how the myth encapsulates the faker's rise and fall, the dangers present for anyone who traffics in signatures.

There's something wonderfully biblical about Andrussier's story. Big Daddy writing on Adam's back is like God signing his first son into existence, if God was a British grappler. (The story also reminds me of Paul Auster, who credited his writing career to a moment from childhood when—after asking Willie Mays for an autograph—he failed to find a pencil: that never happened again.) Feeling the pen's nib on his back, the autograph became imbued with the aura of celebrity, which Adam could access by acquiring more signatures.

"Pace yourself!" warns my own Big Daddy, the egoic voice of discipline that ensures polite conversation. I ask instead about collecting. How one can successfully sell objects that accrue such sentiment? Where do personal investments end and financial considerations begin?

"I have mixed feelings about the autograph business." You can tell from his tone that he has thought carefully about what follows. "I used to have a collector's mentality, but I've sort of killed it off in me. Partly because you cannot really be a good dealer if you are a collector. And a lot of dealers *are* collectors. And then, also, it was something that I recognized was a little unhealthy, something that I needed, maybe, to figure out." This would have been a natural place to change the subject, but Adam's insightful remarks—his willingness to talk about killing off parts of himself (something we all do, but few discuss)—encourages me to press: "Figure what out?"

"[Collecting autographs] feels like a form of denial. I think it is denial of death: the idea that if you can keep collecting these objects that you are somehow defeating death. It's like armor. The more of this stuff you have, the less likely it is to happen to you. A sort of thrill seeking: like, I'm alive but all of these people are dead. I've kind of gone to the opposite extreme now."

Signatures have always been tangled with a desire for permanence, for a life lived beyond the frail and failing body, for something like, well . . .

Immortality.

A Victorian State of Mind

While signatures have existed since before the invention of writing, the popularity of autograph collecting is somewhat new. A distinctly Victorian preoccupation, it collates three wider, nineteenth-century interests: an ongoing awareness of the thin membrane between line and letter, the budding hope that graphology might develop into something like psychology, and an insatiable cultural and colonial appetite for sorting the world into discrete collections.

Writing about the aura that came to surround autography in the nineteenth century, Gerard Curtis argues that this period was marked by "a popular desire to see and collect these original marks and traces for their cachet value."[3] Here I should note that for most of its history, the word "autograph" referred primarily to any handwritten document; only in the 1800s does the sense of "autograph" as a signed name become dominant. What was it about handwriting, specifically the autograph, that captured the popular imagination?

In the era of the typewriter, textual reproduction expanded from printing presses to the domestic sphere. Gramophones and film cameras began to capture the body's unique impressions, challenging the *autographic* claims of alphabetic writing. The first audio recorder was called a *phonautograph*. Early pioneers in photography marketed the technology as a replacement for writing: one of Henry Fox Talbot's original images featured his own script, while Johann Heinrich Schulze's chemical experiments with photoactivity used solar light to write names on chalk.[4] When these new media became feasible and available, people began to dwell on the value of handwriting and autographs, energizing something personal, now under threat.

Letters signify, as do their textures. Writing at the end of the nineteenth century, Walter Crane, artist and illustrator, described how drawn lines are a language, even before they form letters: "line is capable not only of recording natural fact and defining character, but also of conveying the idea of movement and force, of action and repose; and, further, of appealing to our emotions."[5] Crane's interest in the line's signatory potential is part of a longer tradition, stretching back through the wavy marks of Corporal Trim's cane—that creates a "looping signature" across the pages of Laurence Sterne's *Tristram Shandy*—to the painter Protogenes, who recognizes his rival, Apelles, by a cryptic calling card: the inimitable thinness of a single, painted stroke.[6] ("Apelles could not have left a more satisfactory signature," thought William Hogarth.)[7] When these lines cohere into an autograph, the letters denote a name, but their shapes are repositories for a different kind of meaning: an invocation of emotion, character, and inner life.

"At the root of the Victorian fascination with collecting autographs . . . is the potential of autograph to signify subjectivity," writes Samantha Matthews.[8] She locates the zenith of this cultural attitude in the 1870s and 1880s, when a genre of blank novelty book appeared on the market. These empty albums allowed amateur autographers to collect the signatures of their acquaintances. One imprint, titled *Secret Signatures of my Friends*, used blotting paper technology to capture wet signatures written on external sheets. "This little book is intended to be a sort of secret Treasury for safe keeping of our Friends Signatures," reads the preface.[9]

The Victorian autograph book houses a kind of signature that feels delicate, fragile. This autograph is not a confirmation; it is "a fetish that needs protection to escape misappropriation or abuse."[10] To give your signature to another entrusts them with a mark that possessed an extraordinary imaginative power in the nineteenth century. Perhaps that's why *Secret Signatures of my Friends* encrypts its contents: the blotting paper captured autographs as reversed imprints, requiring a mirror to return the signatures to their original state.

Reading Character

While our signed names carry personal feeling, they also communicate character. In Philip Roth's *My Life as a Man*, Nathan Zuckerman gets dressed down by his father. "The nine-year-old had been feeling self-important and the signature showed it." Seizing a school booklet, on which his name is signed, the father yells: "Goddam it, boy, *this is your name*. Sign it *right!*" Later, Nathan does just that, emerging from his bedroom with a well-graved specimen. "Ah, now *that's* a signature! *That's* something you can hold your head up about!".[11] What changed? The "shoulder" on one of his *n*'s? An "arm" of the *e*? The "ear" on his *r*? Letters are formed from elements named after parts of the body. A few small adjustments to handwritten characters may impact how others imagine Nathan's physical and moral character.

Autograph books and graphology became popular in the same decades. The study of handwriting, graphology is one of several, interconnected systems that try to correlate an individual's character, appearance, and moral core. The first of these was physiognomy (face reading), which gained widespread recognition between the 1770s and 1880s through the work of Swiss pastor Johann Kaspar Lavater. Physiognomy, phrenology, chiromancy (palm reading), dactylography (the study of fingerprints), and graphology all share a central belief: that the unseen state of a person's soul makes itself manifest through their physical body in the form of readable signatures. The opening of Joseph Conrad's *Typhoon* (1902) demonstrates the conceit. Captain MacWhirr "had a physiognomy that, in the order of material appearances, was the exact counterpart of his mind: it presented no marked characteristics of firmness or stupidity; it had no pronounced characteristics whatever; it was simply ordinary, irresponsive, and unruffled."[12] I bet his handwriting was forgettable too.

An 1880 photography book entitled *Physiognomy Made Easy* details the facial signatures of inner character. Full cheeks accompany impulse control issues, while a "broad open brow" is characteristic of a love for society.[13] A penny manual on phrenology and physiognomy published in 1887 details other correlations. Small chins, like those possessed by David Livingstone and Oliver Cromwell, indicate force of character, while a large mouth connotes grossness and sensuality. Eyes are particularly nuanced. If round and open, they evince honesty, intelligence, and generosity. When wide apart and oval, like the eyes of Mary Queen of Scots, the person is probably prideful and selfish.[14] "It isn't only that his cheekbones are high," explains a character in Rebecca West's *The Birds Fall Down*, "he's got the Slav signature on his face"—an acute example of the dangerous practices and ethnic categorizations that physiognomy promotes.[15]

Just as facial features become signatures of personal character, handwritten *characters* were thought to contain something beyond alphabetic content. Lavater recognized this, but did not flesh out a theory of interpretation: "The more I compare the different handwritings which fall my way, the more am I convinced that handwriting is the expression of the character of him who writes."[16] Looking back on the nineteenth century, Walter Benjamin glosses graphology as a kind of early psychoanalysis, which "has taught us to recognise in handwriting images that the unconscious of the writer conceals."[17]

The first significant graphological study during this period was published by Edouard A. P. Hocquart in 1812, a disciple of Lavater. (There are older European books on handwriting, such as Camillo Baldi's 1625 *Trattato*, however.) This genre began to proliferate in the 1870s, popularized by *The Mysteries of Handwriting: The Art of Judging Men from Their Autographs* (1872) by Adolphe Desbarrolles and the Abbé Jean-Hippolyte Michon. Shortly afterward, *The Philosophy of Handwriting* (1879) by John Henry Ingram appeared in English. Adopting the nom de plume of Don Felix Salamanca, Ingram analyzes dozens of signatures from figures such as Charles Darwin, Victor Hugo, Stéphane Mallarmé, William Morris, and Émile Zola. The text is both a graphological manual and an autograph book, a genre Edgar Allan Poe contributed to through a series of published investigations, concluding that "a strong analogy does generally and naturally exist between every man's chirography and character."[18]

To take just a few more examples: J. Harington Keene's *The Mystery of Handwriting: A Handbook of Graphology* (1896) offers lessons on how to recognize sanguine and nervous temperaments through handwriting, as well as subtler qualities such as aspiration, avarice, coquetry, lucidity, and tact. In *Graphology: How to Read Character from Handwriting* (1904), Simon Arke pairs actual specimens of handwriting with facing pages of analysis. A hook on the letter "b" betrays a prolix conversationalist, while someone who writes closed "s"-shapes is a Janus in business dealings. John Rexford's *What Handwriting Indicates* (1904) features a section on signatures, which, for the graphologist, "may prove a gold mine or an ash heap."

Rexford privileges the signature for its illegibility and spontaneity, claiming that "the more unstudied the writing, the more truthfully it reflects the character of the writer."[19] In her history of American handwriting, Tamara Thornton builds upon this idea, drawing the useful distinction between speech and gesture. "For handwriting romantics, the gesture of handwriting was a revelation, even a betrayal of the innermost self."[20] Graphology revises the idea that the unconscious is structured like a language. In handwriting analysis, the unconscious appears as calligraphic ornament.

* * *

It's a mistake to think that graphology disappeared after the *fin de siècle*. Take the case of Donald Trump. On January 14, 2013, he tweeted: "I am a handwriting analyst. Jack Lew's handwriting shows, while strange, that he is very secretive— not necessarily a bad thing." This augury was prompted by Barack Obama's nomination of Jacob Lew for Secretary of the Treasury. Lew's illegible signature briefly became newsworthy—it looks like the trail of a whirling dervish, whose feet have been dipped in ink.

Obama joined the fun. "I had never noticed Jack's signature," he said at the nomination announcement, "when this was highlighted yesterday in the press, I considered rescinding my offer to appoint him. Jack assures me that he is going to work to make at least one letter legible in order to not debase our currency."[21] As Treasury secretary,

FIGURE 1

Lew did indeed revise his autograph. The mark debuted on a batch of $5 bills printed in 2013: there the first and last name are clearly demarcated and—while "Jacob" remains ambiguous—"Lew" is almost indisputable.

Are you surprised that Trump puts stock in signatures, affixing his autograph to stimulus checks? He made his name (quite literally) by branding TRUMP across towers. Unlike past presidents, who used A. T. Cross pens, Trump prefers magic markers—specifically, a custom Sharpie: it carries his yellow signature on its barrel, bossed in ormulu ink ("So, I called up the folks at Sharpie and I said, 'do me a favor, can you make the pen in black? Can you make it look rich?'").[22]

During the 2018 NAFTA (North American Free Trade Agreement) ceremony, Trump's signature dwarfed his cosigners. When Mexico's Enrique Peña Nieto held up his copy of the document, Canada's Justin Trudeau demurred. It seems that Trump may have signed on Trudeau's dotted line, overwriting his allotted space. Is there a better metaphor for American foreign policy? In September 2019, the President brought his marker to San Diego and signed his name across

FIGURE 2

the wall with Mexico, flanked by armed officers. House Speaker Nancy Pelosi would later court controversy by using a silver platter of personalized pens to sign the articles of impeachment—a tradition usually reserved for ceremonies and celebrations.[23]

Comprised of thirty individual strokes, which can take more than six seconds to complete, the forty-fifth President's signature has inspired commentary. Tracey Trussell from the British Institute of Graphologists said in 2016 that Trump's autograph reveals "wild ambition, dynamism, bravery and fearlessness."[24] The autograph led another writer to describe its appearance as "the sound wave of demons screaming."[25]

Criminal Signatures

In the realm of criminology, physiognomy and graphology were quickly appropriated into tools for discipline and control. The body's haptic borders have long been theorized as where the soul comes into conflict with society (Nietzsche→ Foucault→Butler), where the inner and outer worlds are forced to reconcile. In other words, the skin's surface is a place where desire meets law.

Physiognomy and graphology began as quasi-occult practices—best remembered by the enduring reputation of palm reading—but they were soon taken up as forensic techniques; the Italian criminologist Cesare Lombroso was an early adopter. Remembered for many wild theories, Lombroso's work posited that criminality is an inherited trait, which carries biomarkers or *stigmata of degeneracy*. Not only did criminals look different, they looked different in similar ways. Specific physiognomies predicted specific crimes: rapists tended to have jug ears (like thieves), whereas pickpockets are recognized by their small wandering eyes.[26]

In the second edition of his influential *Criminal Man*, Lombroso added a chapter on the "Handwriting of Criminals." Working from a corpus of 407 criminal signatures, gifted to him by the director of the Archives of France and a man he calls "the honorable Lucini, the king's agent in Pavia," Lombroso concludes that murderers, highway robbers, and brigands tend to "elongate their letters, adding curves to the upper and lower extensions." Petty thieves sign their names in a recognizable manner. "In general, the letters are soft and ill-formed, and the signatures are clear and easy to read." Graphology does not differ between male and female "assassins," although members of the latter group are not easily distinguished from "honest but energetic women" (whatever that means).[27]

Lombroso not only invented a flawed system of criminal identification, he helped invent the idea of a criminal soul. Crime was no longer a set of actions that seemingly anyone could perform. It indicated a corrupt moral core, lurking within a legible body, displaying signatures of the defective essence.[28]

Autograph Fever

While autograph collecting has been practiced for centuries—German students in the 1500s used a signed yearbook or *Stammbüch*—it gained considerable traction during the nineteenth century, when collecting became a widespread cultural phenomenon.[29] In 1840, the poet and humorist Thomas Hood published his response to an autograph request.

> Autographs are of many kinds. Some persons chalk them on walls; others inscribe what may be called auto-lithographs, in sundry colors, on the flag-stones. Gentlemen in love delight in carving their autographs on the bark of trees; as other idle fellows are apt to hack and hew them on tavern benches and rustic seats. Amongst various modes, I have seen a shop-boy dribble his autograph from a tin of water on a dry pavement.[30]

Hood's letter ends by saying that, having not been provided a flagstone or bench, he will assume (perhaps incorrectly) that the fan wants an autograph made with ink on paper. Jokes aside, Hood reveals the charged relationship between collecting, autographs, and the material world in this period.

During the 1800s, collectors stole more than magpies and hoarded like squirrels. Whereas the seventeenth- and eighteenth-century "connoisseur" focused on fine art, now it was curios that captured the imagination; mummies, seaweed, and signatures became precious commodities. "Is there any inoculation possible to avert autograph fever?" asked Harry Furniss in 1902.[31] An afflicted collector later replied: "The autograph fever clutches all sorts and conditions of men in its deadly grip."[32] If collectors bisected society, their collections dissected its beliefs. While the connoisseur sought a superlative inventory to match his refined sense of taste, the autograph hunter focused on completeness, a desire enmeshed with wider colonial tendencies.

The *autograph hunter* or *autographomaniac* soon became a recognized type. Thomas Bailey Aldrich, editor of *The Atlantic Monthly*, distinguished the autograph fiend as someone driven by the base desire to accumulate *everything* rather than form a discrete collection.[33] The lawyer Adrian Hoffman Joline slyly called autograph collecting a "nefarious habit," practiced by "pests of great men."[34] Joline's particular flavor of self-deprecation becomes clear, however, when we learn that he published *Meditations of an Autograph Collector*, in which he admits that "the 'profane vulgar' consider me, and all other individuals of my autograph-hunting species, as members of the common horde of semi-lunatics who gather birds' eggs, butterflies, tea-cups, and Japanese sword-guards."[35] Why the particular distain for autograph collecting?

One answer might involve a labor theory of autographic value. The "hunter" poaches valuable time that the signatory would otherwise spend on her craft. During his *Chats on Autographs*, Alexander Meyrick Broadley recounts how Longfellow became persecuted by requests for his signature (at the height of autographic frenzy, the poet was forced to sign seventy times a day). In return for postage and an impersonal request, the "fiend" gets a document that may accrue substantial, uncapped value. Henry James imagined a scene where this culture of celebrity leads to the death of artistry: "I *see*, however, the essence of the thing; and the party at the country-house, and the ultra-modern hostess, and the autograph hunters and interviewers—and the collapse, the extinction of the hero."[36] The collector's goal was "to drink inspiration from original fountains," which often involved deceit.[37] "A name written at the request of a stranger is only about as valuable as the same name stamped by machinery."[38] True value comes from authenticity, which—paradoxically— had to be extracted through trickery.

This does not apply to all autography, of course. James Baldwin, in an essay on playwright Lorraine Hansberry and the success of *A Raisin in the Sun*, recalls a different kind of collecting, motivated by recognition rather than calculation:

> What is relevant here is that I had never in my life seen so many black people in the theater. And the reason was that never in the history of the American theater had so much of the truth of black people's lives been seen on the stage . . . And when the curtain came down, Lorraine and I found ourselves in the backstage alley, where she was immediately mobbed. I produced a pen and Lorraine handed me her handbag and began signing autographs. "It only happens once," she said.[39]

In Victorian autograph hunting, however, a parasitic rhetoric surrounds the signature. Possess the autograph of a famous individual and your worth will track their ascension. Despite the insistence that archives and compendiums are impartial repositories, collecting has always been as much about the collector (individual or institutional) as the material collected. Walter Benjamin makes this point in an essay about unpacking his library. "They need not be past-in albums or family albums, autograph books or portfolios," he writes, "a collector's attitude toward his possessions stems from an owner's feeling of responsibility toward his property . . . *collecting loses its meaning when it loses its subject.*"[40] The autograph collector extends his selfhood through his chosen objects; objects that glow, coallike, with the unique trace of a famous person's self. In images of autograph events, the signature often draws more attention than the person for whom it stands.

During our conversation, Adam described something similar: *the psychopathy of collectors.* "I often find it quite amazing how people don't see that the thing that they collect tells people something about *them.* It invites you into quite an intimate world." Adam's idea might explain the nineteenth-century distrust of autograph hunters. *Autographomania* has always had less to do with the actress, musician, poet, or government official who signed the signature, and more to do with the desires of the hunter, his unique obsessions, often coupled with schemes to profit off the backs of others.

This was especially true of institutions in colonial metropoles, which began to coffer objects from their territories at a frenzied pace in the 1800s. Collections, like handwriting, contain an excess. "These museum collections are not what their collectors took them to be," that is, partial, but well-documented records of societies; rather, "they are complete, although particular, outcomes of individual sets of colonial practices," argue Chris Gosden and Chantal Knowles.[41] While museums in the United States were disinterring indigenous corpses in an effort to perfect eugenic theories of race, living peoples were subjugated by the kind of practices that enabled the autograph hunter's quest.[42]

During North American treaties between natives and settlers in the eighteenth and nineteenth centuries, it was common for treaty commissioners to sign documents with two crossed lines. Tracing a tradition of indigenous resistance, Scott Richard Lyons argues that the sign indicated coercion within a document of consent. "The x-mark is a contaminated and coerced sign of consent made under conditions that are not of one's making."[43] Not merely a mark of illiteracy, the "X" signifies a refusal to recognize the authority of autography. Other forms of signature performed similar functions. Paraphrasing an argument by Chris Friday, Alexandra Harmon recounts how Chowitsuit, a leader of the Pacific Northwest's Lummi tribe, "did not conceive of his signature . . . as submission to Americans' will; instead, the ambitious chief likely believed that he enhanced his personal power by securing an advantageous American promise."[44]

The Founding Fathers viewed their own autographs as rebellious: a signature that emancipates in one context may cause utter devastation in another. John Hancock's signature on the Declaration of Independence—which has become a colloquial term for every American autograph—was stylized in protest against the British Empire, according to one popular anecdote. After signing the document with "exaggerated bravado," Hancock is said to have thundered: "There! John Bull can read my name without spectacles."[45] This story of Cock and Bull may be exactly that, however.

British collectors tended to treat "autograph fever" as an American phenomenon that had spread, like an epidemic, abroad. In a telling display of wit, Oscar Wilde recounts how he employed three secretaries while travelling through the United States: one to receive flowers; another to sign autographs; and a final unshorn attendant to clip trimmings from his locks—something the writer's fanbase occasionally requested. The autographer soon developed a condition akin to carpal tunnel; the hairy secretary went bald at an early age.[46]

The almost interchangeable interest in Wilde's hair and autograph reveals an attitude that I will discuss in the next chapter: born of the body, signatures are secular relics, metonyms of an extended self, what Geoffrey Batchen describes as "convenient and pliable" stand-ins for the memorialized subject.[47] Unlike physiognomy, which requires a representation to preserve its subject of study—achievable through photography, portraiture, or a death mask—the autograph is always already mediated, it is itself a form of mediation, between personal character and alphabetic characters, body and world.

4 THE ORIGINS
OF SIGNATURE

"Architecture in Helsinki!" exclaims the ambassador's assistant, who has reinvented himself as a film executive since I last saw him on Syros. He is visiting us in Finland, where we have moved with haste, after my wife Emma accepted a job offer in artificial intelligence. (The company creates neural networks to analyze images—for example, footprints in forensic photographs: criminal signatures.) Everyone else has advanced; I'm still thinking about squiggles. While we walk beneath the summer's midnight sun, the executive comments on our surroundings: "this is a castle city, one of Miyazaki's worlds come to life."

He is referencing the cartoon quality of *Jugend* aka Art Nouveau. Characterized by bloated proportions and organic detailing, this architectural movement dominates Helsinki's streets. "Ornament is to this house what the signature is to a painting," writes Walter Benjamin during a discussion of the style.[1] The decorative exteriors of these buildings often display an ornamental signature of their inner purpose, recalling a face's physiognomy. On Korkeavuorenkatu, a road whose name sounds like an incantation, we find an entranceway with arches of teeth inlaid across its surface. A dentist's office? I can only hope.

To Astuvansalmi

In 1911—November, believed to be the most brutal month in Finland, when light is scarce and the snow has not yet fallen—the composer Jean Sibelius went for a walk along Lake Vitträsk, just west of Helsinki. He had given up alcohol and cigars, after enduring thirteen operations to remove a throat tumor in Berlin.[2] Clear-eyed for the first time in years, he saw something remarkable: a net symbol, drawn in red ochre, on a rock wall not far from the water.

Viewed at a distance, the painting resembles blood, as if a wounded animal smudged against the stone. The lattice becomes visible as you approach: a complex mesh, leading into filigreed hub. Sibelius called the National Board of Antiquities, reporting the painting, but his message went missing, only later recovered. The composer's discovery is the first recorded encounter with ancient rock art in Finland. Whereas prehistoric paintings had been found in Sweden during the seventeenth century, Norway in the eighteenth, and Russian Karelia in the nineteenth, Finland's pictographs are still some of the most underexplored and conserved in Fennoscandia.[3]

A few months before the discovery, Sibelius completed his fourth symphony, which he glossed as a reaction against the trends of modernity. He had previously gained attention for music inspired by the *Kalevala*: a poem that gathers Finland's oral, folkloric traditions into epic verse (images from which adorn Helsinki's buildings like runes). With his new work, the composer traded myth for reality. Russia had been trying to clamp down on a rising nationalism in Finland—then a Grand Duchy of Tsar Nicholas II's empire—a fervor engendered by consciousness forging projects, such as the *Kalevala*. Europe had become increasingly polarized. And World War I was slouching into view.

The composition is a watershed. At its Helsinki premier, the symphony's discord confused listeners. In Gothenburg, the audience hissed; Americans called the music "ultra-modern," "dissonant and doleful."[4] As with Sibelius's earlier interest in folklore, the Fourth Symphony yokes individual, national, and historical feeling. But musically, it "enshrines all the leading characteristics of style and technique," and so becomes, according to Burnett James, "the kernel of the entire nut."[5] In other words, 1911 marks the year when the composer established a kind of signature. Within this kernel, Sibelius's creative footprint, you can hear the embryonic traces of other works, future and prior, ringing out from its core.

I like to think that Sibelius found confirmation at Vitträsk. Walking along the lake, treading a creative boundary between classical composition and modern inharmony, between his country's myths and its history as a front separating Sweden from Russia, he suddenly saw a glimpse of red. Without warning, a Stone Age composition ambushed the composer: the signature of a distant people, still preserved on shore. More rock paintings were discovered and continue to be discovered in Finland. The most important find occurred on Lake Saimaa in 1968, at a place called Astuvansalmi.

* * *

Drive east out of Helsinki and the city quickly wanes. *Jugend* buildings fade into treed boulevards with look-alike apartments. Youth in high waist trousers are cycling to work, headphones leaned on knotted buns. Green and yellow trams quietly transport quieter Finns. There are some cars, but nothing resembling traffic, and buses merge into lanes like disgruntled whales. But everyone is heading somewhere behind us, increasingly distant and obscure.

Now it's mostly woods, woods, woods. Entranced by the Russian border, a thick purple line on the car's GPS, we turn north after Lappeenranta and enter Lakeland instead. Saimaa flickers into sight through the zoetropic trees. "The pine freshener is *strong* in this car," jokes the executive: the forest becomes so fragrant that it presents as artificial. Europe's fourth largest freshwater body, Saimaa's basin feels like a mangrove, threading 14,000 islands.

To reach the site, you must hike or borrow a boat. We found the path next to a handwritten sign. Glacial boulders are here and there, plopped in the pine forest, as if placed from above with intention. Despite hearing birds from the road, things are silent now. You might jump off the path, as I did, mistaking an exposed root for a snake contorted. The trail narrows to a bridge—formed by planks—fording a strait. We meet no one and see no animals. Yet a wet, oily musk appears on the breeze. After the bridge, there are tread tracks from an excavator, but it is unclear how the machine could have arrived, unless by water. A low escarpment will lead you down to a platform on the lake.

Above there is a large cliff face, which looks like a human skull in profile. Its surface flares into images, thought to be five or six thousand years old: one of the most extensive and well-preserved collections of Finnish rock paintings. There are pictures of elk with beating hearts, primitive skiffs, humanoid figures with stick-like breasts, cross marks, and a handprint, sitting off to the far right: the signature of some forgotten artist.

Who left this mark? And what did she intend? It is astonishing to think about just how long humans have been pressing their painted palms onto stone. So long, in fact, that the first imprinters may have been *not yet human*. In 2018, researchers discovered that handprints in Spanish caves predate *Homo sapiens* by at least 20,000 years. They were, the scientists argue, painted by Neanderthals.[6]

There Is Nothing Funny about Elk

One of this book's recurring ideas: the signature is a place where humans, other animals, and the inorganic mix and remix. The handprint at Astuvansalmi does not indicate a specific person. Its palm's lines are muddled, the contours lost. But it still functions as a form of signature, both of a nameless individual and her species—the wider genetic community.

The handprint also marks a site of interspecies collaboration: a strange, improvised ecology where bodies of stone, lichen, feathers, and skin come into contact. While the ink's exact ingredients are unknown, it is thought to have been made by heating iron oxide with animal fat and blood, possibly incorporating bird eggs as binder. To remain distinct for millennia requires sacrifice, the peculiar chemical properties of avian embryos.

The rock itself seems like a passive surface, yet the handprint endures because the granite secretes a silicate substance. Over time, this has a laminating effect, preserving the ink from harsh weather, a form of mineral memory, a lithic writing pad. In places like Saraakallio, the silica's opacity fluctuates with the seasons. It whitens in summer, glazing the paintings, revealing them once again when the temperature drops. The hand at Astuvansalmi would have long faded if it were only human.

* * *

Several weeks later, I am in Turku, talking to Ismo Luukkonen, who has been photographing rock art since 1994. "I have seen all of the rock art in Finland"—he tells me early in our conversation, with a factuality drained of bravado—"except for the new find." A silver hoop hangs from Ismo's left ear, warmed by his wiry blonde hairline and strong, flush cheeks.

During our interview, Ismo's eyes are wide and fixed, the face of mild alarm or full attention. Now and then, he presses his palms against the table, as if keeping time to a song imperceivably slow. He is patient with my vagaries but does not waste words, speaking with a linguistic economy that, after years of living in Britain, requires readjustment on my behalf. (In England, it's often easier to fill a void than allow something to emerge from its depths.)

But my conversation with Ismo never becomes uncomfortable. Our dialogue mimics how people speak when they look at art. A careful observation (his more often than mine), maybe a reply, before turning back to behold a common object in silence. Soon we are talking about the paintings themselves. I ask about "moose imagery," having learned that Eurasian elk and North American moose are the same animal. I am trying to figure out what handprints have to do with these leggy bulls and cows.

"Elk is the most important figure, or moose, however you want to say," he tells me. "I use elk, because I am not from America, where they have moose. Moose it sounds a little bit funny, but there is nothing funny about elk." At the time I laughed, agreeing that *moose* is odd, doubly so when spoken by deadpan Ismo. Only in reading back over my notes do I wonder if the photographer spoke in parables. Was I the American playing Adam, come abroad to name the animals with reductive terms, *nullifying them as beings on their own account*?[7]

We move on to the most important question: why has Ismo devoted his life to these paintings? What does he find so thrilling? It has to do with *presence*.

> For me, at least, the most important message of those paintings is that they were done so long ago. It is something about touch, for instance. Like this handprint [at Astuvansalmi]. Someone had to touch the rock. And I can go there and—I should not because it is not allowed—but I can touch it too. And, in a way, I can touch the person that made the print. This art is kind of a link between generations.

Dressed in yellow shorts and a crimson tee, it is easy to imagine the photographer scrambling across boulders, on the hunt for pictograms, some so bleached that they can only be seen after processing. Once an image has been digitally saturated, the red hues pop back into clarity. He later demonstrates this process in his studio, a shed behind the house, spilling with archaeological texts and adventure equipment (snowshoes, an inflatable kayak).

Moments after Ismo mentions his enduring amazement, however, he shifts into a darker mood. I am to blame. In an essay, the photographer describes his experience at Astuvansalmi as "almost frightening," "[a] huge cliff and silent landscape."[8] I ask him about the balance of awe and terror. His voice drops: "there are some places that are extra terrifying."

Ismo begins describing Värikallio, a site on the Karelian border, not too far from where the *Kalevala* originates. "When I went there for the first time it was really frightening," he says. "It's in the middle of wilderness, a national park. You go there through the forest and you drive to a place where there is dark water, a cliff, and a platform. The cliff rises straight from the waters. It is a scary place. Something about the atmosphere."

When we later return to the topic of Värikallio he tells me that it was better in the winter, on his second trip, "when everything was clean and white, and the cliff was sleeping in a way." Although speaking figuratively, something serious edges into Ismo's smile. I am starting to believe him about the elk.

The Self, Extended

Signatures create *presence*. This is why I have defined the term broadly, to encompass autographs, handprints, animal tracks, personal inscriptions, and any other marks that point back to a denotable body. I am drawn to signatures because they seem connected to human personality. At the same time, more so than writing, *signature* is a term we use to understand the behavior of other things too. In this section, I explore troublesome ideas from anthropology, ethnology, and sociology that try to make sense of this idea, how a body—of any kind—might scatter throughout the world.

To worship graven images, to touch a signature and feel its pulse, to find emotion in an autograph: all of these ideas trade on an implicit logic, what Edward T. Hall calls *extension transference.* By this he means "mistaking the symbol for the thing symbolized while endowing the symbol with properties it does not possess."[9] To visit a handprint, like Ismo describes, and in doing so forge a connection with its creator, extends a sense of presence from an imagined body to its signature. This kind of transference was once dismissed as a "primitive" mentality, before the entire notion of primitivism became untenable, exposed as a cognitive correlative to colonial projects. (Note how Hall himself calls *extension transference* a mistake.) Could it not, however, be rehabilitated as a way of talking about our beliefs regarding autography?

A similar term is *distributed personhood*, which describes how ritual objects sometimes behave as if they enclose fragments of the self. Alfred Gell calls these relics *excuviae* (imagine horcruxes from the Harry Potter series). A written signature does not symbolically substitute for the human; it is not a metonym, in this argument, but a detached piece of personhood that becomes an agent in certain cultural contexts.[10] A distributed self can easily become a vulnerable self, however. In *Tristes Tropiques*, Claude Lévi-Strauss writes about the Nambikwara, an indigenous people of the Amazon, who keep their names hidden to avoid interference. The anthropologist coaxes a group of children to give up their secrets, "one against the other, till in time I knew all of their names."[11]

A name, in this account, grants power over the named: Rumpelstiltskin rediscovered in Mato Grosso. *Tristes Tropiques* says as much about the actual beliefs of the indigenous people surveyed as it does about the anthropologist's own longings. Instead of "breaking with a Eurocentric model," argues Jacques Derrida in a famous critique, "he reproduced it."[12] (Lévi-Strauss did not know the Nambikwara language, the visits were brief, involved "as much guess-work as field-work," and were intended to discover an authenticity undistorted by modern, urban life.)[13]

In *Tristes Tropiques*, names are treated like exuvial forms, sloughed fragments of the corporal self. Lucien Lévy-Bruhl's notion of *participation* further describes this magical affinity between the body and its signatures. The term "denotes a peculiar kind of psychological connection with objects," where a subject is bound to an object "by a direct relationship which amounts to partial identity."[14]

When writing about Western Australia's aboriginal peoples and the Kai tribe of Papua New Guinea, Lévy-Bruhl gives an example of *participation* in which biological sheddings continue to act upon their issuing body at a distance, like the entangled particles of quantum physics.

"We know that to the primitive mind the hair and beard, as well as the saliva, nail-parings, excreta, undigested food, etc., all form an integral part of the personality."[15] Here biological detritus bears a signature of its origin. Rather than revealing "the primitive," *participation* better prefigures how we have come to think about forensic evidence. How many television crime plots revolve around a lifted fingerprint, the DNA signature of a sloppy criminal, or frame jobs constructed on planted hairs?

For much of the twentieth century, James Frazer's *The Golden Bough* influenced our beliefs about rock paintings—especially handprints. In his massive study of magic and religion, Frazer discusses what he calls *sympathetic magic*, based on the *law of similarity* ("like produces like," that is, "an effect resembles its cause") and the *law of contact* (things once connected continue to "act on each other at a distance through a secret sympathy").[16] The formulation aids Frazer when thinking about names: "the link between a name and the person or thing denominated by it is not a mere arbitrary and ideal association." This kind of magic can affect a person "just as easily through his name" as through "any other material part of his person."[17] While proper names have long been treated as primarily linguistic objects, thanks, in part, to a tradition inaugurated by Plato's *Cratylus*, I follow Frazer by focusing on the material properties of names and signatures.

But Frazer and his successors missed something closer to home. Describing the magic that eluded Frazer as the "magic of the modern—not the primitive—world," Michael Taussig believes that contemporary cultural beliefs involve practices formerly associated with primitivism.[18] I think this is the best way of critiquing the ethnologists above who, far from being impartial observers, were actively seeking their own image or its estranged inversion. Taussig's idea about modern magic holds weight, especially in relation to signatures.

Search "Trump Hollywood Walk of Fame," if your device is nearby. The memorial barely counts as a personal signature; DONALD TRUMP appears in the same block font as every other star, yet multiple people have mutilated the brass text in protest. Even if we try to distinguish between a political attack on reputation and a magical attack on personhood, the practice remains identical. TRUMP has been graffitied with swastikas, stained with blood, stickered over by PRIDE flags, and completely destroyed with a pickaxe. The perpetrator of that final act explained his motive: "as long as that star remains on Hollywood Boulevard, there's going to be a really negative presence there."[19] The *law of contact* and *law of similarity* are far from extinct. Trump's personhood seems to extend into his name; a *presence* can be felt radiating from the signature.

Or imagine a Martian anthropologist, happening upon Grauman's Chinese Theatre in Hollywood, adjacent to the Walk of Fame, where the famous have impressed handprints and signed their names in wet cement. "As a cultural practice the handprint has survived for thousands of years," writes Sonja Neef, "from the images in prehistoric

FIGURE 3

caves to that neo-religious ceremony on the Walk of Fame in Los Angeles."[20] There's some Cinderella logic here: if the palm fits, the cement confirms identity. Marilyn Monroe impersonators have been photographed with their hands hovering over her dried prints and autograph. And the ceremony is surprisingly accepting of nonhuman signatures: the pawprints of Uggie, a Parson Russell Terrier made famous for his role in *The Artist*, can be found at the Theatre; Herbie, the Volkswagen Beetle from *The Love Bug*, left its tire tracks too.

Cave Signatures

All paths lead to animals. The rock paintings at Astuvansalmi are not nearly as old as those discovered in France and Spain, where images have been found—some composed more than 64,000 years ago—at Lascaux, Pech Merle, Maltravieso, Gargas, El Castillo, or Chauvet. Yet the themes remain recognizable. There are handprints in caves and on cliffs all across the world (most impressive, perhaps, is Argentina's Cueva de las Manos, where swarms of palms reach out of the past). The prints share walls with large animals, like the elk at Saimaa: ibex, bison, horses, aurochs, deer, mammoths, bear.

Archaeologists once speculated that the proximity of handprints to animal images indicated a form of hunting magic, after Frazer. Summarizing these theories, Sarah Minor likens cave paintings to murderous ideation: the "Paleolithic hunter made her first kill on the walls of Lascaux to prompt the kill incarnate to present itself on the hunt . . . together the figures display a chorus of individual hopeful voices, of unique signatures moving in a pack."[21] The coupling of signatures with sympathetic magic surfaces again and again, despite thin proof.

The claim arises from evidence of touch—images at Pech Merle interweave handprints and horses, for example, and the palm at Astuvansalmi looks impressed onto a giant skull, as if its painter tried to massage the sinuses of a sleeping god. It is understandable why an archaeologist's mind would default upon the haptic. But hunting? "There are no paintings of realistic hunting scenes in Lascaux or in any other cave in Europe that we know of. So why make this reference?" asks Nicolás Salazar Sutil.[22] The trope reveals more about the beholder than it does about the object beheld, especially regarding our contemporary estrangement from animal life.

Georges Bataille had little sympathy for sympathetic magic. In his book on Lascaux, the philosopher offers another theory. For him, the images represent not only the birth of art and the human, but also sacred prohibition. Hunting engendered feelings of transgression; cave paintings of animals present a cleave in human consciousness. "Every animal is in the world like water in water"—they "still inhabit the land of immanence from which the human being withdraws," writes Oxana Timofeeva.[23] In other words, ancient handprints might have always been as enigmatic as they are today: early humans, like modern spelunkers, were reaching back toward something that had quietly slipped away, trying to emmesh their signatures with a world withdrawn.

* * *

If you have heard of Chauvet, it may be thanks to Werner Herzog, whose *Cave of Forgotten Dreams* premiered in 2010 to critical acclaim. At the heart of the Chauvet mystery, we find prints. Interviewing Dominique Baffier, a scholar of paleolithic culture, Herzog listens as she describes the signature of one ancient artist. "He has a slightly crooked little finger. And that's extraordinary, because it gives a physical reality to a prehistoric individual." It grants *presence.* They follow his handprints and soon we see the preserved impressions of an extinct predator: "the longest cave bear tracks currently known in any cave."

A crooked finger may project "physical reality," but it also creates the possibility for performance. Consider the caves of Gargas—where many handprints display missing or shortened fingers, spawning conflicting theories. "Frostbite!" some say. "Ritualized amputation!" counter others. Where most see unwitting communication, Thomas Macho finds

FIGURE 4

performance: "the fingers of those [mutilated] hands that had been placed with their back against the rock were bent inward and, in some instances, retouched and shortened afterwards."[24] Signatures change form, medium, and meaning across time, but still preserve certain operations. The handprints in Gargas are signatory writing, "in so far as every imprint follows and repeats the principle of difference."[25] They allow a person to control how he is recognized and remembered through patterned declarations of allegiance and dissent.

There is data here, but it's noisy—any clean signal has been distorted by the latency of history. Yet many have tried to retrieve it. When confronted with the deep past, writers reach for the idea of *signature* again and again. "Why this feeling of presence?" asks Maurice Blanchot. Describing the human figure at Lascaux, he calls it: "the first signature of the first painting."[26] The handprints themselves read like autographs for archaeologists, revealing a hard-wired human impulse. "It presumably served primitive man as a sort of personal symbol, a kind of signature."[27] And Judith Thurman refers to Chauvet and its neighboring caves as places "where early Europeans left their cryptic signatures."[28] While it is interesting to postulate what these marks meant, it is equally fascinating to watch onlookers project their own ideas back onto the stone like shadow puppets, unable to make true contact with what lies beneath.

In another memorable scene from Herzog's documentary, scientists delayer a wall of images and impressions. The oldest traces on the stone are scratches from cave bears. On top of these curving claw marks, a person drew a mammoth. "The archaeologists were not surprised to find bears' claw marks on the walls," reports Georges Didi-Huberman; "it was more surprising for them to discover copied bears' claw marks, engravings made by men or finger drawings."[29] A simple sign of humanity—five fingers and a palm pressed onto stone—becomes an opportunity for interspecies reflection: how a painted hand dragged across a surface makes the shapes of other animals. Herzog's documentary depicts something like an epistolary palimpsest, transmissions between animals and humans. After the mammoth dried, the wall was later scored again by other bears, as if these animals were responding to the painted prey.

Discovering the footprints of an eight-year-old boy next to those of a wolf, Herzog asks: "did a hungry wolf stalk the boy? Or did they walk together as friends?" Despite these overlapping imprints, the clear symmetry between boy and beast, handprint and bear paw, Herzog continues to represent Chauvet's paintings as distinctly human. But the more time I spend looking at palm printing, the more it begins to seem like a technique borrowed from animal tracks rather than an aesthetic awakening; a way of extending the body, outward, consciously or unconsciously. "To make something its own, the body knows how to leave some personal stain," writes the philosopher Michel Serres. Offering a list of different kinds of *stains*, which include sweat, aroma, and excrement, he then connects these acts to the signing of signatures: "my signature looks sweet and innocent, seemingly unrelated to those habits. And yet . . ."[30]

Herzog's collected filmography reflects a wider tendency to quest after ethnographic authenticity. *Cave of Forgotten Dreams* might arise from a moment, recorded in his *Fitzcarraldo* journal, when the director stumbles upon Asháninca signatures in the Amazon, not far from where Lévi-Strauss ventured. "On the gravel bank I saw stones into which the Campas have scratched their names." It is an uncanny encounter, which makes Herzog feel as if he is in "a concert hall where a little-known orchestral work is being performed."[31] Or, perhaps, within a cave, surrounded by images, both alien and familiar: a symphony heard long ago, like Sibelius encountering the net at Vitträsk.

During the documentary's conclusion, we are shown one of Chauvet's "negative" handprints, overlaid with WERNER HERZOG. Curiously, only positive impressions are displayed during the film; it is not until the closing credits that the camera fixes on a palm's empty outline. "To create these distinctly human marks . . . early artists blew crushed pigment directly onto the bare stone between their five spread fingers—perhaps a kind of signature, a symbol of their existing this way, or at all."[32] Contrasted with Herzog's written name, this negative handprint becomes an allegory for interpreting the mysteries of cave painting: the empty space that we fill with speculation, whose true content will always be lost to the past.

Seals and Signets

While cave prints remain speculative signatures, something closer to our modern autograph appeared later. These marks predate the alphabet. One story goes like this: twelve thousand years ago or so, hunter-gatherers began farming in the Fertile Crescent. Agricultural cultivation gave rise to trading networks. Debts accrued. The books had to be balanced.

These peoples invented a rudimentary accounting system with small clay tokens: spheres, cones, tetrahedrons, and disks. Once crafted, the tokens became a type of stamp. Impressed into the side of a wet clay envelope—a jug, box, or similar container—the tokens were then sealed within. The envelope held a debt; its exterior recorded the contents. Eventually someone realized: if we do away with the envelope, signs themselves can store value. (There are objections to this theory, of course.)[33]

While tokens tracked debt and credit, they did not assign ownership. What use was a piggy bank of figurines if it could not be swapped for food? Enter signatures. When goods were transported, they were first placed in baskets and sacks. These enclosures were sealed with a unique mark, impressed upon a tag, designating the sender or recipient, with a geometric, animal, or anthropoid image.[34]

Reviewing one trove of seals recovered from the Tepe Gawra site in Iraq, archaeologists became puzzled by the lack of human primacy. "Anthropoids and animals are treated uniformly . . . none of the figures emerge as more or less significant than the next."[35] It's tempting to make a claim about the prehistoric relationships between humans and animals, or to liken the seals to cave paintings. Both seem to come from a world where people and creatures dwelt within a common field. These feelings intensify when one examines the images. They are full of beautiful, spare figures that are not-quite-human nor fully animal. Bird heads are affixed to long-legged bodies, limbs akimbo; a crouched person swirls amid some kind of gazelle; in one of the most cryptic examples of the anthropoid variety, the figure seems to split apart at the joints, ready to recombine with other forms: animal, vegetable, or mineral.[36]

Recent signatures incorporate similar themes. Ernest Thompson Seton, writer and founding member of the Boy Scouts, drew a pawprint when he signed his name; Kanye West's autograph occasionally contains a bear; the novelist Bryher, partner of Hilda Doolittle, signed her letters with a griffon. Kipling poked at this tradition:

> Sir,—The following is the kind of thing that greets me at the end of most of the letters which I daily receive:— "I have the honour to be," &c. &c. followed by a design in ink which might be meant to represent three snakes' tails and a set of triangles. "Very sincerely yours"—a felled fir-tree with a shower of chips about the stump. "Yours sincerely"—a Greek Theta, and a thing like a dead cat.[37]

5.1

5.2

5.3

FIGURE 5

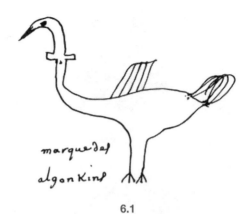

marque des
algonkins

6.1

haronhiateka

chef dusault.

6.2

FIGURE 6

While these examples are cute and personal, other animal signatures are cultural markers of individual and collective identity. Native American tribes, especially those in the eastern woodlands, signed treaties with totem signatures in the eighteenth and nineteenth centuries.[38] The Great Peace of Montreal, a treaty signed between France and thirty-nine First Nations in 1701, provides a particularly striking example of the practice, containing totem signatures of birds, foxes, beavers, rats, and other animals.

Jumping back, phonetic writing did not emerge until around the third millennium BCE. According to a popular theory, the alphabet arose from farming: agriculture breeds culture.[39] A number of subsequent thinkers have tried to connect the origin of the alphabet and agriculture with the rise of monotheism, monogamy, and patriarchal societies, a project as controversial as it is seductive.[40] (And recently challenged by findings at Göbekli Tepe and elsewhere.)[41]

The alphabet still encodes a cryptic fascination with the natural world. What began in caves and on cliffs is remembered by handwriting. While our ancestors impressed handprints onto paintings of mammals, we sign our names with letters derived from similar imagery. According to enduring—if wobbly—theories, the Latin letter "A" descended from the Greek alpha, which came from the Phoenician *alp* or *aleph,* originally an ox hieroglyph. Flip it over to reveal the creature's horns: ∀. "D" may originally have been a fish in an elongated, pictogram form; "N," a snake. And "K," from the

Greek kappa and Phoenician *kaph*, corresponds to a glyph representing the handprint.[42]

We form autographs out of symbols, abstracted from crude sketches of animals and handprints. One researcher specializing in "lateralized cognitive processing" speculates that hieroglyphs depict the left side of an ox because bovines are calmer when processing visual information on that side of their bodies.[43] (While drafting this chapter, I met an Argentinian horsebreaker in a Cambridge pool hall: she said the laterality also applies to stallions.) If "A" arose from our relationship with cattle—a nuanced understanding of their cognitive faculties—then what does it mean that we subsequently used the same letter to brand these beasts of burden with our mastering mark? Or, in the most despicable moments of history, to brand each other?

5 SIGNING THE BODY

A wedding in Moscow. The art appraiser and an American correspondent, my old friend. It is a big affair, full of artists and journalists, reeling from postnuptial joy and the day's political events. That morning, thousands of people gathered to demand that opposition candidates appear on the ballot for the city's Duma elections. And so, amid a klezmer band and champagne toasts, the journalists huddled near power outlets, filing stories about the brutal police.

Of the hundreds of guests, there is an even split between nationalities. At first, nerves. Early in the evening, I overhear an American discuss how she purchased a "burner phone" for the trip to protect herself from . . . well, I'm still not sure. But by the end of the night, we had all blended into one communal whole, hands joined together, dancing hora circles around the bride and groom, who were lifted up and down in wooden chairs, howling like children at the rollercoaster's crest.

Crowned by a halo of seedpods tipped with gold, the bride wore a dress she had designed herself. It was thick like canvas and embroidered with text from the Jewish *ketubah*,

FIGURE 7

a sacred prenuptial agreement, literally a "written thing." It ends like a contract. *To this covenant we affix our signatures.* The *we*, it turned out, meant *us*.

After the ceremony metallic markers appeared, and at her invitation we began signing. Initials, autographs, and handprints manifest across her body. Some scribbled their names alone, others inscribed wishes, prayers, and lines of poetry. Soon the *ketubah* had been cosigned by everyone. The dress became a document of beauty before our eyes. The protestors never got their candidates' names on the ballot.

* * *

The signing of bodies is an old practice, sometimes erotic, often entwined with the painful distribution of power. It takes some work to disentangle acts of affinity from baser tendencies. (A warning: this is a difficult chapter, which includes discussions of slavery, violence, and sexual assault.) Both in the ancient world and during the Middle Passage, slaves were tattooed with the names of their owners. Free men and women were forcibly branded and then retroactively claimed. Signatures did more than signify servitude: they produced the conditions necessary for enslavement.

The mark of the master can annihilate identity. In the third century BCE, Bion of Borysthenes called his father a man with "no face to show, but only the writing on his face, a token of his master's severity."[1] Brands like these literally efface someone's physiognomy, *overwriting* their biometric signatures. "There were those countenances that resembled a palimpsest," writes Nancy E. van Deusen, describing victims of the sixteenth-century Spanish trade, "the letters of a former master's name partially erased or scraped off, and other blackened letters carved over the crevices."[2]

Generations later, the slaver's signature becomes an injunction against genealogical inquiry. "I am told that there are Haitians able to trace their ancestry back to African kings," recounts James Baldwin, "but any American Negro wishing to go back so far will find his journey through time abruptly arrested by the signature of the bill of sale which served as the entrance paper for his ancestor."[3] Barriers to the past, signatures overshadow the future too. While Greek tragedy depicts children haunted by parental stigma, there may have been a belief that stigmata, tattoos, and other brands could be biologically inherited.[4]

But in another way, *they can be*. While the budding field of epigenetics remains controversial, some scientists want to suggest that children exposed to trauma in the womb carry "a particular chemical mark, or epigenetic signature, on one of their genes"; others worry (rightly, I think) that claims like these invite eugenic interventions.[5]

Writing about the branding of black female bodies in North America, Hortense J. Spillers wonders if "the phenomenon of marking and branding actually 'transfers' from one generation to another, finding its various *symbolic substitutions* in an efficacy of meanings that repeat the initiating moments."[6] Hank Willis Thomas examines a similar substitution, focusing on black men. His art series *B®anded* explores "how black bodies were branded as a sign of ownership during slavery, and how their descendants' bodies are branded today through corporate advertising."[7] Blackness became a visible commodity during the slave trade;

"branding was a dehumanizing process of classifying people into groupings," writes Simone Browne.[8] If the signatures found in cave art are marked by continuities between animals and the human, branding exploits this continuity in reverse.

And it is ongoing. Victims of sex trafficking are tattooed unwillingly, producing a form of "psychological enslavement" via "names and symbols," resembling brands "used to mark ownership over cattle and other animals"; a few years ago it was revealed that the "self-help" sex cult NXIVM incised its female members with the initials of a Master.[9]

Victims of signatures are dehumanized, but have not always been human. Herodotus recalls how, during his invasion of Greece, the Persian king Xerxes built a bridge, spanning the Hellespont. Soon after, a storm destroyed the structure and infuriated the king. He ordered his men to tattoo the strait, as if even the sea might submit to a sign. "Bitter water," they said, "this is your punishment for wronging your master when he did no wrong to you. King Xerxes will cross you, with or without your consent."[10] Is this a true story? Or a clever narrative display of hubris, foreshadowing the King's eventual defeat at Salamis? Xerxes would have benefited from a conversation with John Keats, whose epitaph in a Roman cemetery reads: *Here lies one whose name was writ in water.* Even the most enduring human signatures are eventually dissolved, like names etched on melting ice in Chaucer's "The House of Fame."

Signatures are bridges; crossing requires consent. Consider two adolescent acts of inscription: cast signing and drunk shaming. In the first instance, autographs are collected on the plaster covering a broken bone, as if the signatures might join together to protect an injured peer. In the latter example, names and derogatory utterances are inscribed onto someone incapacitated by alcohol. During the coverage of the sexual assault of Audrie Pott—which took place while she was unconscious—and her subsequent suicide, reporters focused on how an assailant had written his name on her body, followed by the locative "was here."[11] The signature can both shame and protect, strengthen and violate.

Violence and signatures are connected like a Möbius strip. To sign a person without consent is a horrific act of disempowerment, which often accompanies other forms of bodily harm; other forms of bodily harm can rob a person of their perceived claim to a signature. Poet Eileen Myles recounts how, after being raped as a teenager, she walked down to a nearby beach and wrote her name in the sand. "EILEEN MYLES. Yes, that's who I am. I rubbed it out with my foot."[12] In other cases, there is nothing to rub out: the autographic act becomes infeasible. Lea VanderVelde tells the story of Milly, Harry Dick, and William—former slaves of David Shipman, a soldier in the Revolutionary War—who sued for their freedom in 1820s Missouri after being recaptured by opportunists. All three people seemed to know how to sign: their autographs appear on legal documents. "Sadly, in later filings, however, after being held in jail for some time, they do not write their names again."[13] Either they had forgotten how to write, the historian thinks, or something prohibited them from doing so.

I Am You

Branding the body with a tattooed name has seeped into popular culture, recuperated through the rhetoric of eroticism. In "Free Spirit," hip-hop artist Drake raps his refrain in the imperative: "Tat' my name on you so I know it's real."[14] The speaker wants his addressee to validate her commitment, making their relationship "real" with a tattoo.

Drake does not administer the brand—he's aroused, instead, by visibility and reputation. The song features Rick Ross, who, in a track with Meek Mill, likens his signature to erotic currency. "Went from poor now women screamin' for my signature."[15] If there is an inequality here, it arises from the lopsided display of desire. Although Drake later promises that he will *be yours*, he declines to mark himself and expose his skin to pain.

Even without explicit violence, these lyrics feel barbed. One explanation may involve generic conventions. Rap has a history of imagining the signature as a territorializing tool. This is a borrowing from graffiti culture, where nominal *tags* claim public space for an individual or her crew. In "Hold On," 50 Cent rhymes: "Used to do graffiti, now look: we major / Don't make me write my name across your face with a razor."[16] The locations of these signatures differ but share a common need for prominence and visibility, related to the optics of shine, studied by Krista Thompson.[17] "Came to represent and carve my name in your chest," says Method Man in his aptly titled "Bring the Pain."[18] Lil' Kim threatens to carve her name *in your face*; Afu-Ra chooses the head, because it will make his name akin to memory; and M.O.P. swaps blades for bullets, shot in the shape of a signature, *across your belly*.[19]

Like a tagged train car, the human body becomes contested territory in a battle of signatures, marked by dynamics related to the visibility and surveillance of blackness in America. If another common trope of hip-hop is the power of invisibility, captured in the common boast *you can't see me*, this kind of signature works like a protective proxy—a rapper's way of exercising "control over his own image by denying everyone else's access to it," except via the autograph, tattooed on a surrogate body.[20]

Drake's idea is slightly different. He wants the addressee to write *his* name on *her*. Razors and machine guns are unnecessary. The fantasy rests on erotic control, crossed with a desire for reputation. It's closer to Big Pun's verse on Digital Underground's "The Mission," where a tattoo affirms intimacy in blunt terms—"I never call you slut . . . that's why my initials is on your butt"—or Young Buck's attempt at seduction: "I'm visualizing my name tattooed on that ass, baby."[21] But it is hazardous to separate these (supposedly amorous) male fantasies from their violent intensification, described with courageous, nauseating detail in Michelle T. Clinton's poem "Anti-Erotica": "he carved his name & left semen that stinks & drips out slow."[22] Here hip-hop opens onto a wider literary tradition.

Observe the metaphysical John Donne. His poem "A Valediction of my name, in the window" (c.1600) prefigures Drake's song—both share the belief that an inscribed name makes you *be there in spirit*. The signature becomes a surrogate body in the literary imagination, allowing one to remain spiritually present in the event of physical absence, another kind of extended self. In this poem the signature claims a female host, leeching off her vitality.

> My name engrav'd herein,
> Doth contribute my firmnesse to this glasse, [. . .]
> 'Tis much that Glasse should bee
> As all confessing, and through-shine as I,
> 'Tis more, that it shewes thee to thee,
> And cleare reflects thee to thine eye.
> But all such rules, loves magique can undoe,
> Here you see mee, and I am you.[23]

Donne's voyeuristic poem begins when an unnamed speaker carves his name into a lover's window—perhaps, scholars think, with a diamond ring designed for writing. (Donne and Gang Starr's Guru share a taste in jewels: "I rock diamonds that cut glass out of window panes," raps the latter).[24] The poem's speaker imagines that, should he die, his lover will look into the inscribed window. The mirror shows "thee to thee," allowing the woman to see herself, but with a parasitic addition. Donne's name overlaps his addressee's face, like the master's mark on Bion's father. She sees herself, emblazoned with *his* sign: "Here you see mee, and I am you."

This fantasy is creepier than its hip-hop equivalent. Compare Donne to Big Pun, who, in cypher verse, creates a strikingly similar image. "I'm carving my initials on your forehead / So every night before bed / You see the BP shine off the board-head."[25] Pun's image depicts forced perception; Donne's fantasy involves coerced possession. The signature not only shines upon the woman, it threatens to assume her selfhood: *I am you*. Donne's erotics recall the branding of slaves. Discussing Iberian slave markets during the 1500s, a historian quoting Trinh T. Minh-ha sounds eerily like the poet: "the surface of the skin exhibited the master's name, in effect saying, 'I am you, not me.'"[26] Killer Mike foregrounds the subtext here: "forehead engravers, enslavers of men and women."[27]

Later in Donne's poem, the woman takes a new lover. When she receives a letter from this man, however, the window superimposes her old beau's signature onto the page, obscuring the letter's true author. Then, when she tries to reply, the name intervenes again, redirecting her prose to the poem's speaker. If only for a window blind! The letter arrives at its destination, but not the one its writer intended. Donne anticipated what hackers call a "man-in-the-middle" attack. This exploit relies upon the forgery of digital signatures, allowing a third party to eavesdrop on the messages between two entities, who believe that they are communicating through a private connection.

Erotic Inscription

Why is the signature, especially in its tattooed and branded forms, so often associated with violence, power, and erotic control? Inscription approximates penetrative sex; tattooing simulates it on the body. When branded by another, the body reflects the *microphysics of power* to which it is subjected. When a person marks herself, however, the signature can become a *second skin*—a way of protecting the body by encasing it in pigment, displaying unseen characteristics or values through certain visible signs.

Of course, not all tattoos and brands are signatures. And the same mark can carry different connotations based on the individual and her community. There is a long-standing equation, however, between writing and sexual power. Friedrich Kittler describes this as an omnipresent metaphor, which equates women with a white, virgin sheet "onto which a very male stylus could then inscribe the glory of its authorship."[28] I want to turn now to two examples, from visual art and film, where male signatures emblazon women's bodies toward differing ends.

Cut short by his death at thirty, Italian artist Piero Manzoni's career explored the artistic potential of his body's signatures. A creative flurry in the early 1960s questioned the value of impressions and excretions. The *Works of Verification*, for example, simply feature Manzoni's fingerprints, stamped in ink, set alongside alphabetic grids, recalling dactylography's roots in criminological verification and the idea that letters find their origins in the sensual world. A few years earlier, Manzoni created *Breath of the Artist* by blowing into balloons attached to autographed plaques. In *Artist's Shit*, he canned his own excrement. The instructions for this last performance were simple. Weigh the cans and sell them at the price of gold.

In the works described above, it is tricky to gauge sincerity. The economics of art are tied to an artist's aura, the perceived value of his signature. Was Manzoni's mission to manipulate the market, creating value seemingly *ex nihilo*? In this sense, he succeeded where the alchemists failed, extracting gold from leaden waste. Or did the artist want to teach us something serious about the body's ability to infuse matter with spiritual material: to perform, revising Coleridge, a repetition in the *finite body* of the eternal act of creation? In doing so, Manzoni ensured a kind of life after death—for his *oeuvre* doubles as a reliquary.

This thematic exploration of the body's signatures, both autographic and excremental, culminated in the *Living Sculpture*s (1961), when Manzoni signed human bodies, transforming them into works of art. The "statues" were accompanied by a certificate. "Mr. /Mrs. [the signed subject] has been signed by me and therefore has to be considered an authentic work of art."[29] While famous men were also signed— such as Umberto Eco, Emilio Villa, Marcel Broodthaers—the photographs documenting his performance feature mostly nude, nameless women.

FIGURE 8

Manzoni appears erotically gleeful in contrast to the female figures. The documentation has a voyeuristic quality. These women's breasts and torsos are on display, but their faces are cropped or turned away. Bodies reduced to busts: fleshy doublings of the *Winged Victory of Samothrace*. If a participant's certificate was yellow, it meant that only an arm, leg, or torso would be transformed into art, disarticulating a body into parts, like the *blazon* tradition in literature.

Manzoni casts himself as a regretful Pygmalion. Rather than converting stone into flesh, he reverses the transformation. It feels generous to read the tone as ironic, a send-up of Western art's traditional male gaze. Manzoni's own gaze seems to betray complicity rather than critique: the grin is puerile, his pen almost priapic.

As long as signatures have been tools of domination and control, however, they have also been used to reclaim the body's agency. But to seize the pen, and its associated power, does not necessarily make inscription any more equal: it merely reverses who is signed and who does the signing. Is there a truly equitable model for the erotic signature? Or is the very act predicated on a sense of imbalance, a violence at the heart of writing?

Peter Greenaway's *The Pillow Book* (1996) explores this question and its sexual implications. The film is based on Sei Shōnagon's *Makura no Sōshi*, an eleventh-century record of life in a Japanese court. The book rings with lyric intensity. After reading it, Maggie Nelson confessed how she felt "at once the need to die and be reborn one thousand years ago."[30] Shōnagon frequently alludes to calligraphy and how it facilitates intimacy and violation. "I also find it painful to be scolded by someone when I have been peering at his calligraphy. This sort of thing does not happen with a man one loves," she writes.[31]

Greenaway's film opens on a child's face, perfectly still. A hand calligraphs her skin. We hear: "When God made the first clay model of a human being, he painted in the eyes, the lips, and the sex. And then he painted in each person's name. Lest the owner should ever forget." The camera reverses to show her father, a Big Daddy, carefully wielding the brush. We learn that this is a birthday ritual, between father and daughter, creator and creation. "If God approved of his creation, he brought the painted clay model into life by signing his own name." The child turns around. He signs her neck.

Time passes and Nagiko is now in her twenties. She works in Hong Kong as a model, speaking the Mandarin learned from her mother. A particular erotic preference has taken hold: Nagiko asks lovers to calligraph her body, signing their names on her skin. Freud himself could not have dreamed up a more fraught case study. In *The Pillow Book*, sexual conquest is a form of autograph collecting. "I was determined to take lovers who would remind me of the pleasures of calligraphy."

Like Donne's carefully orchestrated cuckoldry, Nagiko prefers to *top from the bottom*: her submission becomes a veiled form of domination.[32] One day she meets an Englishman, a translator of four languages, who writes

"Jerome" on her forearm in ugly, block letters. She gives him a second chance. This time, he inks her chest with French and Yiddish, but the letters lack sensuality. This is not writing, she informs him, only scribbling. He suggests that they reverse roles. Nagiko becomes indignant. "How can I get pleasure writing on you? You have to write on me!" She eventually agrees, however, discovering her own graphological talent.

The Pillow Book demonstrates how the signing of signatures can both enforce and upend inequalities stemming from religion, gender, race, and imperialism. In a city historically occupied by both Japan and Britain, Nagiko's sexual radicalism eroticizes colonial relationships. (Greenaway's film was released shortly before the British handover of Hong Kong.) "I am going to be the pen, not just the paper." Greenaway troubles the idea that we can solve power imbalances by simply changing who signs what—that the master's tools can dismantle his house. In this world, someone must always submit to the signature.

The film ends in blood and gore. After Nagiko deprives the translator of her calligraphy, he suicides out of desperation. She signs his corpse. Without permission, a publisher flays the man's skin and binds it into a book. She then kills the publisher in a revenge plot. By becoming "the pen," Nagiko also inherits a painful legacy inseparable from inscription.

Watching *The Pillow Book* in 2019 thickens its message, but also rehabilitates the signature's revolutionary potential. With protests surging through Hong Kong's streets, a story catches my ear: it is about Cantopop singer Denise

Ho, a figurehead for the democratic resistance to Chinese encroachment. She has been autographing the protestors' gear—hard hats and protective goggles—as if her signature might toughen the thin barrier between brain matter and rubber bullets.

Autographic Skin

Outside of art, it's even more taxing to judge bodily signatures. This has created trouble in law and medicine. During the summer of 1994, a woman named Julie Wilson went to the doctor. She complained of a burn on her backside. Preparing to salve the wound, Dr. McKenna noticed something strange: the burn formed two capital letters: an "A" and "W." He phoned the police and Mrs. Wilson's husband, Alan Wilson, was soon convicted for assault occasioning actual bodily harm by Doncaster's Judge Crabtree.

A year after his conviction, the case surfaced again in the Court of Appeals. It came to light that only the doctor and an arresting officer had given testimony in the original trial. This time around the assailant had something to say. Mrs. Wilson had asked for and consented to her husband's signature. As he recalled in the initial police report:

She wanted me to give her—put my name on her body . . . I think her exact words were [something] like, "I'm not scared of anybody knowing that I love you enough to have your name on my body," something of that nature, and between us we hit on this idea of using a hot knife on her bum.[33]

The appeal was granted, with the argument that Mrs. Wilson consented (and was able to consent) to Mr. Wilson's branding. The court case is of interest to legal scholars for it questions to what degree an individual can agree to harm before the state must intervene. From a cultural perspective, Alan Wilson's account brims with assumptions and beliefs about the autographed body.

Would Dr. McKenna have called the police if the scars formed the letters "JW" instead of "AW"—an indication that Julie signed her own body? Why did Judge Crabtree privilege the testimony from the medical and disciplinary authorities? And why have I been unable to find testimony from Mrs. Wilson? Was there a sense that the signature, somehow, spoke for itself?

Similar questions were already circulating in the medical sphere at the end of the nineteenth century, during the discovery of a malady called *dermatographic urticaria*. For those afflicted, the soft touch of a finger will create persistent welts. Because the irritation is localized, appearing only in the places where contact has been made, it becomes possible to draw fine lines and letters.

"[G]ranted a proper epidermis and a specially susceptible nervous system," Jeremy Broome wrote in an 1897 article for *The Strand*, and "you will be able to make upon your own or somebody else's body any signs, inscriptions, or marks which caprice or imagination may suggest."[34] Broome goes on to tell the story of John Miller, whom he calls *the man with autographic skin*, and describes how hysterics are particularly susceptible to graphic symptoms. The author fails to note the sinister side of these signatures: how the medical establishment used dermatographia to control female bodies.

This practice flourished in one particular clinic: the Pitié-Salpêtrière hospital in Paris, under the direction of Jean-Martin Charcot, a founder of psychiatry. In order to test a patient for the condition, doctors would often sign her body. As Toussaint Barthélemy recounts: "A patient is hypnotized; the doctor writes his own name on the patient's forearms with a rubber stylet and issues the following suggestion: 'This evening, at 4pm, after falling asleep, you will bleed from the lines that I have drawn on your arms.'"[35] Noting that the male doctors would often sign and date "their" skin writing in preparation for photography, Vicky Kirby asks who, in fact, can lay claim to the marks: the doctor or his patient? What issues the autograph? The doctor's stylus or the receptive surface of a patient's reactive skin?[36] Like Nagiko, the woman absorbs the signature and then appropriates it as her own. Her skin becomes a transcript of resistance.

While I continued to look at the words on the flushed skin of her inner arm, the distance between me and the doctors in the Salpêtrière closed. Medicine had granted permission to a fantasy that men have never abandoned, a muddled version of what Pygmalion wanted—something between a real woman and a beautiful thing . . . The name inscribed on Violet's arm was still visible.[37]

This passage from Siri Hustvedt's novel *What I Loved* shows how the medical fantasies of nineteenth-century physicians are not lost to the past. (Hustvedt's novel draws on the research of her sister, Asti Hustvedt, whose work recovers the stories of Blanche Wittmann, Augustine Gleizes, and Geneviève Basile Legrand, women who formed the canvas for their male doctors' signatures, institutionalized in the Salpêtrière Hospital and largely forgotten.)[38] Occasionally these simmering fantasies bubble to the surface. Simon Bramhall, a liver transplant surgeon at Birmingham's Queen Elizabeth Hospital, pled guilty in 2017 to assault by beating. His crime? Burning his initials into patients' organs. Using an argon beam and a steady hand, Bramhall would sign his subjects, leaving a signature inside of their bodies.

The public reaction has been surprisingly mixed. The advocate group Patient Concern argued that it "is a patient we are talking about, not an autograph book." On the other hand, a former patient of Bramhall's argues that the procedure causes no lasting damage to the liver and heals over quickly, calling for him to be reinstated, "so that he can save more lives."[39]

* * *

Throughout the fall, Mariel Bayona and I have been trading letters. Based in San Francisco, she holds an MFA in sculpture, co-founded the Bass & Reiner Gallery, and works as a tattooist, out of the Mission District's Black & Blue parlor. Mariel is concerned with the line, its balance between perfection and personality. "In tattooing, given all the traditional technical rules," she tells me, "a tattoo artist's goal is to reach and dominate a perfect line. However, there is a beauty in an imperfect-human-made line that eventually makes and shows the artist's signature and trademark." After reading and writing about tattoos, it's increasingly odd to be unmarked. And so, with an upcoming trip to the Bay Area, I book an appointment—an absence on my left arm itches for ink.

I am drawn to Mariel's work for its hybridity. A self-described "border child," born in the United States, raised in Mexico, treading the space between Juárez and El Paso, she draws creatures that inhabit other kinds of borders. She calls the figures Tescuani ("beast" in Nahuatl). Not-quite-human nor fully animal—reminiscent of the images on Sumerian seals—these figures, she says, emerge from her subconscious, made accessible through automatic drawing, repetitive processes of patternmaking, not unlike the repetitions of a signing hand.

Over several months, I send her autographs, passages from this book, reproductions of cave paintings, and esoteric quotations about the relationship between animals and the origin of the alphabet. To my relief, she is unfazed. "I must say I have been waiting for a project like this for a while."

The studio itself was founded by Idexa Stern—who relocated from Germany in the '90s to study with Angela Davis—as a safe place for lesbians in the S&M community, which operates with an ethos of radical inclusion. Stern's philosophy is as captivating as Mariel's own. Discussing why people wear tattoos, she invokes terms that recall ideas like mystical participation, distributed personhood, and the laws of contact and similarity. "It's more an awareness that there's an unseen world, that there are things that we strive towards," says Stern, describing a form of knowledge learned from "so-called 'primitive' cultures": "like if there's a mark, and if there's blood, if there's an intention, you can really move some energy."[40]

When I make my way to the shop in November, two tourists are waiting in the reception area—done up in nautical décor—conversing à la Abbot and Costello. They want geographic coordinates tattooed on their forearms and ask for the name of an artist who takes walk-ins. "Who," replies the receptionist, repeatedly, in reference to a tattooist who goes by Who. Confusion ensues; you can imagine the scene.

Mariel greets me with a hug and reveals her sketch. (We had agreed that, aside from my initial prompts, I would not be involved in the design.) It's a fantastical creature, something between an ox and an elk, whose horns wrap up into abstract letters signed by a gracious, curling hand. The rest of the session became a blur, however, with endorphins galore: the belated realization that needles are scary stuff. As we near the end, I finally open my eyes. Because of the chair's position, my arm is out of sight, but I can see Mariel's face, framed by dark bangs, which radiates the satisfaction of an artist completely absorbed in her work. "Are you happy with how it turned out?" I ask. "Is it that obvious?"

Selfishly thinking that I commissioned something personal, I had also, simultaneously, become a canvas for the expression of someone else's personality. The tattoo is a shared signature—here voluntary, but often coerced and devastating. In my case, the design contains an encrypted reference to its artist's name, a hidden autograph, which remembers the violent history of inscription. When asked about her tendency to depict sharp horns—such as those that now adorn my left arm—Mariel notes how her surname comes from toponyms like Bayonne and Baiona, etymologically tangled with the word *bayonet*. "I try to put that element in my drawings," she says.[41]

6 SIGNALING DIGITS, DIGITAL SIGNATURES

"Every human being carries with him from his cradle to his grave certain physical marks which do not change their character, and by which he can always be identified . . . These marks are his signature, his physiological autograph, so to speak." Or so claims Mark Twain's "Pudd'nhead" Wilson, who uses fingerprint identification to prove identity in a court of law.[1] This chapter examines different kinds of *physiological autographs* by exploring how signatures are recorded, detected, and verified. While handwriting provides one method for linking a body to its marks, a person's voice, face, and fingerprints can also serve as signatures, but necessitate a technological capacity to read and reproduce these biometric identifiers—a history inseparable from imperial and state power. In the end, I turn my attention to the promise of digital and electronic signatures, which offer safer modes of verification.

Writing Machines

The word "polygraph" refers to both a mechanical device for copying handwriting and a type of lie detector, one that measures physiological changes during interrogation. Thomas Jefferson used the first type of polygraph; his model had a mechanical arm that, when attached to his pen, created a scalable copy of a handwritten document in real time. Writing technologies complicate the primacy of signature. If Jefferson signs his name with the polygraph, does his original signature, somehow, become more valid than its reproduction, even though original and copy are coeval? Or is he capable of signing two documents at once?[2]

The writing machine transcribed letters but also graphic noise. In this way, both kinds of polygraph tie the human body to a written record of bodily information. Steven Connor thinks that the criminological polygraph's data can be read through an enlarged sense of *signature*, in both a biometric and textual sense.[3] Lie detectors, like graphology, rely upon an equation between the appearance of writing (lettered or otherwise) and unseen character.

Few remember the *teleautograph*. Elisha Gray's machine debuted at the 1893 World's Columbian Exhibition. The invention consisted of potentiometers and a metal plate that when written upon transcoded handwriting into a series of electrical signals. This telegraphic information could then be sent long distance to a receiving stylus that would recreate the handwriting with minimum delay, implementing a spatial juncture between original and copy.[4] "Handwriting and signatures were finally moving through the wires."[5]

Another device proved longer lasting. Robert DeShazo acquired the rights for the Autopen during World War II. It does not transmit handwriting, but instead stores templates of its users' signatures, which it traces with a pen affixed to cams (early versions stored the "master" on a turntable matrix, while newer models are digital). Autopens can sign hundreds of times per hour. They even make it possible to put signatures on ice, as it were.[6] In 1965, the collector Charles Hamilton believed that Madame Tussaud's waxworks would soon come equipped with Autopens, signing tourists' autograph books with ghostly transmissions from beyond the grave—an example of what Richard Grusin calls the signature's *premediation*.[7] The signing machine complicates forgery. If *you* trigger the Autopen to sign your name, it is not a fake; yet the same sign, activated by another, would be an instance of deception.

Where exactly does the difference reside? Have you ever been asked to print out a document, sign, scan, and email it back to your tormentor? Why the hesitation over using the many suitable and acceptable forms of electronic signature? Surely a scanned reproduction is as much of a "copy" as pasting in a signature from another document? Something like the *law of contact* still governs our belief in the autograph. Hand to pen to paper → an unbroken chain of presence.

Adopted by US presidents like Lyndon Johnson and Richard Nixon, the Autopen is chiefly a time-saving device, reminiscent of Roman signatory stamps or the French monarchical practice of authorizing secretaries to sign important documents.[8] Yet the Autopen remains shrouded in mystery because its vendor respects their customers' anonymity. "You do your own research," DeShazo told a visitor to his plant who inquired about famous users.[9] (Hamilton took up the challenge, concluding that JFK used six different robot signatures.) "I always heard the autopen was the second-most guarded thing in the White House after president," reported a member of Bill Clinton's staff.[10] Imagine: a Secret Service for signatures.

While legally binding, these automata autographs continually unsettle witnesses. Travelling abroad in 2011, for example, Barack Obama made international headlines by using an Autopen to sign a piece of legislature—supposedly a historic first. The act was quickly challenged by US Representative Tom Graves, who questioned the legal basis for signing in absentia.[11]

Beyond partisanship, I think that people find the Autopen and its many iterations disconcerting because of mimetic perfection: it does the job *too well*. By reproducing signatures without variation, the Autopen swaps similarity for exactitude. The mechanized signature abolishes a kind of correspondence between the signer and her sign. Handwriting records our real-time physiological signatures (my own autograph seems to vary with coffee consumption), even if these conditions cannot be faithfully decompressed and interpreted.

The Autopen's controversy stems, then, not only from a machine playing surrogate, but from a machine recreating a signature that is out of sync with the signatory's current physiology, her body noise.

What the machine lacks, it borrows from elsewhere. Autopen operators can unknowingly fold themselves into someone else's autograph. "I just drew a deep breath," said one operator, interviewed on the job, "it was enough to change the signature."[12] The authenticity of Kennedy's automated autographs points back to the Autopen operator, not the president: "each secretary eventually injected his own personality into every Kennedy imitation."[13] And the machine has its own signature too. When pushed to top speeds, older pens would sign slanted vowels. "Or if the pen is fastened in the holder too low, there may even be an extra flourish in the signature . . . Definitely this machine has got a mind of its own," believed one secretary.[14]

The Autopen haunts two artworks that think about repetition, identity, and mechanization. For *Signature* (1993), Tim Hawkinson bolted a crude pen to a school desk, creating a kinetic sculpture that signed his name ceaselessly for weeks, piling spindled autographs on the gallery's floor. "But no matter how dogged this machine's assertion of self, its final effect is anonymous, futile."[15] Agnieszka Kurant's *The End of Signature* (2015) begins with futility and champions anonymity to think about collective labor practices—the end of singular authorship. Encouraging visitors to her exhibit at New York's Guggenheim to sign their names on blank sheets,

FIGURE 9

she then scanned the pages and used an algorithm to create a
"crowd-sourced communal autograph," fed into an Autopen
inside of the gallery and projected onto the museum itself,
"signed and resigned in perpetuity."[16] The piece was first
installed on a public housing project in Utrecht, writing the
residents' amalgamated signature on the building from left
to right, "as though an invisible hand was signing the wall
over and over again," democratizing the magical writing
at Belshazzar's feast and the invisible hand(s) of economic
theory.[17]

Typewriter

The vibrancy of handwritten signatures emerges at a historical moment when the unique movements of the human hand become eclipsed by the impersonality of typewritten script.[18] Discussing this moment, Friedrich Kittler quotes Franz Kafka's letter to Felice Bauer, where he confesses a hesitancy to sign documents and his preference for type. "I also sign everything (though I really shouldn't) with FK only, as though that could exonerate me; for this reason I also feel drawn toward the typewriter in anything concerning the office, because its work, especially when executed at the hands of the typist, is so impersonal."[19] Kafka employs two methods of encryption. Using initials instead of a signature provides an expert in handwriting recognition less evidence with which to draw conclusions about the graphological characteristics of the signatory. By dictating speech to a typist, Kafka hopes that his hands are doubly mediated. Although a typewriter does provide some anonymity, even this machine generates a signature, which can be traced to a specific individual.

Arthur Conan Doyle popularized the idea. In "A Case of Identity" (1892), Sherlock Holmes discusses writing a monograph on the subject of "the typewriter and its relation to crime." He believes that "a typewriter has really quite as much individuality as a man's handwriting. Unless they are quite new, no two of them write alike. Some letters get more worn than others, and some wear only on one side."[20] Sherlock Holmes would have delighted to learn about "keystroke dynamics," the biometric technology that promises to identify a computer user by the unique rhythm and pacing of her typing.[21]

Film

Ismo's earlier comment about his desire to touch a handprint, and, by doing so, connect with its creator, reminds me of another encounter: the opening of Charles Dickens's *Great Expectations*. Visiting the graveyard where his parents are buried, Pip describes how he never saw his parents or their images—"for their days were long before the days of photographs." His sense of physiognomy and personal character derives, instead, from the alphabetic characters on their headstones. "The shape of the letters on my father's, gave me an odd idea that he was a square, stout, dark man, with curly black hair. From the character and turn of the inscription, '*Also Georgiana Wife of the Above*,' I drew a childish conclusion that my mother was freckled and sickly."[22] By making contact with these inscriptions, the boy believes he can somehow commune with the persons they represent.

In *The Missing Ink*, his ode to the art of handwriting, Philip Hensher sounds a lot like Pip. "Observed the difference between Mummy's handwriting, nice, cosy and round . . . and Daddy's, elaborate, graceful, reaching upwards boldly and with a signature like a knife into a wound . . . Insight grasped: people don't write all the same and the way they write is a little bit like them."[23] Graphic style can be a kind of crypt: the textual *corpus* becomes a surrogate body, a parsable corpse. Pip's reference to photography is not accidental. Walter Benjamin argues that photography—and, by extension, video—marked a turning point in the history of identification, which had previously relied upon a handwritten signature for authentication. "Photography made it possible for the first time to preserve permanent and unmistakable traces of a human being."[24] This vaporous statement gets at the heart of a fetishism implicit in photography, how it extends the self's iconic *presence*, challenging the signature's indexical claims.

When hunting celebrities, the selfie has superseded autography. It makes *presence* more explicit, less forgeable, by connecting two physiognomies, interweaving their physical signatures. We might return for a moment to where this book began: cathedrals and signatures. Fifty years after Orson Welles made *F for Fake*, fifty miles northeast of Chartres, Notre Dame caught fire. Were you online? Did you see the response? Pictures surfaced from family holiday albums, study abroad, trips booked on the promise of imagined feasts—selfies, portraits, and Polaroids, posed in front of Notre Dame. Personal notes accompanied these posts on Facebook, Instagram, and Twitter. Stories and outpourings. Outpourings and emojis. *Après Notre Dame, les émoticônes* . . .

"It took 200 years to build, and just hours to burn down 😵"

"mon coeur est en larmes 😣"

"Can't believe it. My dream is ruining before my eyes 😭😭😭 #NotreDame"

"And yes it would have been nice if there were sprinklers though! And yes she definitely burned very quickly, since the majority of the wood inside was 800+ years old! 😞😅😭😭"[25]

It is easy to be cynical (that last comment, with its lopsided balance of elegy and technical critique, reminds me of the darling William McGonagall—sometimes anthologized as history's least successful poet—who, when called upon to memorialize the 1879 collapse of Scotland's Tay Bridge, versified the engineers' failure to buttress its central girders). And yet the posts about Notre Dame are generically cohesive and exemplify an increasingly common reaction to tragedy, an emotional strategy that should not be dismissed out of hand.

What does it mean that the collective response to catastrophe is a selfie? In Victor Hugo's *Notre-Dame de Paris*, the archdeacon holds a printed book, gazing toward his medieval cathedral with trepidation. *Ceci tuera cela,* he says: *this will kill that*. Hugo understood how new media technologies leach vitality from older forms of representation (the novel is set in 1482, shortly after the printing press came on the scene, when, Hugo thought, texts first supplanted ecclesiastical buildings as the storehouse of public knowledge).

Glancing between our smartphones and the flaming church in 2019, we had the opposite take: *this* can save *that*. While Notre Dame burned, we doused the flames with pixelated tears. We wrenched a representation out of the church's materiality, bound it to our digital selves. It's the same message, said in manifold ways. Some of that was *mine*. I left my own mark *there*. And took part of it with me. Here is the proof.

A specter pervades these images. Composed of joyful, smiling faces, unaware of the impending future, they become retrospective portents, what Roland Barthes called "the imperious sign of my future death."[26] The realization that we are rapidly receding from a captured moment—as we face backward in contemplation—has always been photography's *shtick*. "Photography is the inventory of mortality," writes Susan Sontag; yet the selfies upend expectations.[27] While the fires raged, flesh had the potential to outlast mortar. (I ran this theory by the Los Angeles filmmaker, who thinks it is too charitable. "These selfies are just the movie *Titanic* with flatter affect. Tragedy becomes the package for selling a face.")

Gramophone

Other machines extend signatures beyond the visual. The gramophone had the ability to both read and write—it could inscribe the human voice in a quasi-textual form. Phonography's grooves made people question, argues Lisa Gitelman, "how some inscriptions might or might not be like texts."[28] Writing in 1927, Bertrand Russell thought that vocal signatures would one day replace handwriting as a method of authentication. "Perhaps, instead of legal documents, we shall have gramophone records, with voice signatures by the parties to the contract."[29] It's a popular trope for science fiction and spy movies. In *2001: A Space Odyssey*, "Voice Print Identification" identifies characters arriving at a space station, while in the original *Mission: Impossible* Ethan Hunt performs his famous set piece—a silent cable drop into a white, high-security vault—because it is considered easier than bypassing the required retinal scan and voiceprint identification.

Like many forms of signature, the gramophone record's grooves became meshed with colonial visions of subjugation and control. "Within the first decade of sound reproduction, we find evidence of a Western political fantasy of imperial phonography, whereby the phonograph is imagined as a tool capable of harnessing the voice to literally establish colonial rule and political allegiance during the Scramble for Africa," Renée Altergott, writing a doctoral dissertation on the subject, told me in correspondence. "A single oath sworn orally before the machine was to be reproduced—or even wielded—at will, to effectively colonize further territory through sound." This idea, in various forms, becomes a nefarious technique used across the history of signatures. Like the name tattoo, which can both arouse and enslave, technologies of personalization and preservation are always vulnerable to being harnessed for biometric oppression.

Almost a century later, we are now starting to implement this kind of technology. Her Majesty's Revenue and Customs (HMRC) rolled out its Voice ID program in 2017—allowing the voice to be used in place of a password to access tax records. These *voiceprints*, as they are known, have been glossed as "a form of biometric identification and authentication, as sensitive as a fingerprint."[30] The program came under criticism for gathering *voiceprints* without user consent, which violated EU (European Union) data laws, and forced the authority to delete five million records. HSBC implemented a similar system in 2016, allowing users to access their bank accounts using vocal security. Again, the system proved fallible: a BBC reporter's twin gained access to the account, using only his voice.

Fingerprinting

In recent years, Apple has popularized biometric identification. Between 2013's iPhone 5S and 2017's iPhone 8, Touch ID became a standard technique for unlocking the devices with a fingerprint. Here technology encodes assumptions inherited from criminology and anatomy. As early as 1788, J. C. A. Mayers declared "the arrangement of skin ridges is never duplicated by two persons."[31] Anticipating the gramophone's *inscriptions*, the discourse surrounding fingerprints also imports graphic metaphors. Henry Faulds, writing during the 1910s, argued that the skin's lineations resemble letters.[32] Faulds records how in the absence of seals certain Babylonian and Chinese scribes would use their fingers to notarize tablets and wax. Not until the twentieth century, however, does technology make it possible to truly "read" the finger's signatures.

Fingerprint identification arose as a form of colonial regulation, developed by William Herschel in the late nineteenth century. While employed by the Indian Civil Service, Herschel used the forensic technique to prevent the repudiation of handwritten signatures.[33] In addition to populations of European colonies, fingerprint identification eventually targeted other people of color, the poor, and citizens classed as degenerates and prostitutes. "The desire to identify, and therefore control, these 'suspect' bodies," writes Simon A. Cole, "is what fuelled the demand for identification technologies."[34] As part of the Criminal Tribes Act in the Indian Code of Criminal Procedure, colonial officials began to designate entire populations as potential offenders based on visible features.

The promise of fingerprinting as a revelatory science faded into a tool of identification, the way that graphology pivoted into handwriting recognition. Recently its authority has been further challenged: the 1990s opened onto an era where fingerprint forgery entered into the popular imagination and *point counting*—a standard method for fingerprint matching—was deemed unscientific, replaced by David Ashbaugh's *ridgeology*. Most damning of all, no one knows for certain whether fingerprints are unique. Pudd'nhead Wilson may have deserved his name.

Apple has phased out Touch ID from iPhones, using Face ID instead. This tool may prefer certain mugs. Inheriting physiognomy's tendency to exaggerate and categorize bodily differences, the Face ID's recognition system faced backlash. The device was thought to be optimized for white faces; reports surfaced that Chinese family members are able to unlock their relatives' devices. Apple responded with a statement assuring that the technology was trained on "a representative group of people accounting for gender, age, ethnicity, and other factors."[35] As with the colonial history of bodily signatures, however, what appears to be a "representative group" can often be laden with political, historical, and ideology biases.

Electronic Signatures

To understand the controversy arising from digital and electronic signatures requires knowing more about the legal history of authorization. In the Anglo-Saxon period, English grants of land and rights were typically signed by various witnesses, each inscribing the sign of a cross, invoking religious authority. These crosses were not necessarily written by one's own hand: the personal autograph had not yet consolidated authority. When Edward III signed his name in a 1362 letter to the king of Castile—which historians believe indicates that autography was already a long-standing practice in Iberia—"the autograph confirmed but did not replace the king's seal."[36]

For many of the centuries that followed in England, seals and autographs existed in a reciprocal relationship, but the seals held true authority. Legal scholars point to the Statute of Frauds Act of 1677 as the moment when handwritten signatures became an officially recognized element of contract law, but other experts note that autographs had already gained significant legal power by the sixteenth century.[37]

Before autography consolidated authority, seals offered checks and balances. Henry VII, for example, signed his will with: his great seal, privy seal, a signet kept by his secretary, and another object, featuring an eagle, held in his private possession. Disconnected from the body, a seal's authority stems from possession of the impressing matrix. In order to counteract forgery—a lost signet or manufactured duplicate—multiple seals could be used in the presence of witnesses, ersatz notaries. Pendant seals were attached by parchment tags and silk cords: authenticating countersignatures, materially preserved.

Jump ahead in time and we find a different world: many modern legal frameworks distrust the seal, and, instead, equate the signature's authority with handwriting's perceived presence: "seals and stamps were replaced once more by signs of the body."[38] There are numerous examples, but, when signatures have been challenged in US and Commonwealth courts, judges are surprisingly forgiving about the shape, form, or material of an autograph, so long as it accurately represents intent.

To wit: *Morton v. Copeland*, an 1855 English case, ruled that a signature need not even include a name, so long as the handwritten mark is recognizable. The consensus crossed the Atlantic. William Wirt, US Attorney General, set a precedent for extreme flexibility in 1842, when he wrote that "a signature made with straw dipped in blood would be equally valid and obligatory."[39] But all examples like these share a common idea—the signature flows, like blood, from a person's body.

Given this flexibility, why are modern courts harsher when it comes to using seals as an alternative to an autograph? A revealing statement was made by Sir John Strange in 1754: "that sealing is signing, I am not convinced; for sealing identifies nothing; it carries no character."[40] Here, perhaps, you can anticipate my argument: modern legal frameworks draw the same presuppositions as graphology, which inherits older ideas about the distribution of selfhood. There must be *character*; a chain that links back to an originating body, cosigned by voice, touch, or some other watermark of presence.

Seals, however, transfer the body's authority to a matrix. Stamping a matrix creates little performative difference, no recognizable *character* communicated from the impressing hand. But Japanese law, for example, has no issue recognizing seals. To this day an individual might have different types of matrices, known as *hanko*, to impress their sign (*inkan*). *Jitsuin* seals are more formal and binding—registered at a government office—whereas *mitomein* are casual, used for everyday purposes.[41]

When it comes to the use of digital and electronic signatures, which do not rely upon biometrics, you can still find an analogous skepticism. First, however, we need to distinguish between the two terms that are often conflated in discussions of the topic. Electronic signatures refer to any process whereby a signature is appended virtually (think signing PDFs), whereas "digital" signatures indicate protocols involving encryption and verification. The latter technology often secures the former. Electronic signatures inherit earlier concerns about reproduction, which take us back to Jefferson's use of the polygraph.

Notably, in 2016, a California bankruptcy judge ruled that the DocuSign platform—widely used to electronically sign documents—did not constitute a legal replacement for an autograph. In his memorandum, Judge Robert Bardwil asked: "what happens when a debtor denies signing a document and claims his spouse, child, or roommate had access to his computer and could have clicked on the 'Sign Here' button." The *clicking* seems to be the problem, which, in many ways, remediates the *stamping* of seals. In other words, it lacks *character*. None of this would be an issue, Bardwil thinks, "had the debtor simply signed the documents in his own handwriting."[42] I am not so sure.

Handwriting identification—like the larger history of biometrics—remains controversial. Some critics are hesitant to agree that "forensic document examination" even qualifies as a legitimate practice.[43] The sea change in US forensic law began with what is referred to simply as *Daubert*. The 1993 ruling of *Daubert v. Merrell Dow Pharmaceuticals, Inc.* replaced the *Frye* standard, a case that set precedent for the admission of scientific evidence. (*Frye* involved systolic blood pressure measurement to measure deception, a precursor, as it happens, to the polygraph.) The new standard privileged indirect scientific evidence over conclusions "generally accepted" by a scientific community, the basis of the previous standard.

Daubert replaced *consensus* with *reliable principles and methods*. This cut a pathway for challenging handwriting analysis. While forensic document examination has a certification program, academic journals, and other trappings of science, its methods are not necessarily empirical.

The challenge came in *United States v. Starzecpyzel* (1995), which revolved around stolen art and the forgery of signatures. Judge Laurence McKenna reviewed the evidence in favor of handwriting analysis and rejected the practice's scientific claims. In a crafty proviso, however, McKenna then argued that, for this very reason, handwriting analysis should be exempt from *Daubert*, as it is unscientific. Instead he likened the handwriting analyst to a harbor pilot, who has innate knowledge of fluid dynamics and oceanography, but cannot necessarily explain how he steers his vehicle in scientific terms.

There's some evidence that forensic verification works—attributing two signatures to the same hand, for example—but handwriting experts are often called upon to perform less straightforward tasks, which move *recognition* toward *graphology*, such as attributing authorship from both forged and authentic signatures or detecting disguise attempts.[44]

There has been a sustained attempt to apply science and mathematics to handwriting in the court of law, best remembered by Alphonse Bertillion's belief that a person's script corresponded with the handwriting of their parents, and philosopher C. S. Peirce's testimony, chronicled by Louis Menand, that forgery could be detected by applying probability theory and statistics to signatures.[45] In the nineteenth century, the Dreyfus Affair, Tichborne Trial, and Parnell Commission are important moments in the history of forensic identification, when signatures—autographic and biometric—captured the popular imagination. There are better methods for verification, once we leave behind the handwritten autograph and decouple signatures from the indexical body.

* * *

Digital signatures can involve different types of protected communication, but many rely upon public key infrastructure (PKI), which facilitates asymmetric encryption. This sounds more complex than it is. In asymmetric encryption, two "keys" are generated for each party: one public, one private. Users swap public keys and use them to encrypt their messages. Once sent, the message can only be opened by the recipient's private key, which is never shared.

But how do you know that someone is who they say they are? Digital signatures, like their handwritten equivalent, require a third party. There are different schemes for linking public keys to individuals. *Certificate authorities* are the most popular, which act as a kind of name registry, verifying that a party has the right to use a given key. Multifactor authentication might be introduced, necessitating another form of confirmation, like a USB token, relinking the chain to a body or an item in its possession. Digital signatures that use key encryption resemble medieval chirographs, in which a contract, written twice, was subsequently torn down the middle. Each party then possessed a copy, which could only be "made whole" if reconnected to its other, serrated half.

When it comes to using digital signatures to underwrite electronic signatures, legalizing a signed PDF, for instance, there are several frameworks in place that implement ISO standards, making electronic signatures adhere to regional laws. A PDF can be edited, its data changed. In order to combat this, electronic signatures implement timestamping, which certifies the integrity of a document at the moment of signing and keeps a record of when the signature *went live*.

Issues arise around long-term validity; timestamps can rely upon certificates, which need to be confirmed by a third party. If, at some future date, the certificate authority goes bankrupt, how, then, can the original signature be verified? Some address the issue by using multiple timestamps (recalling the multiple seals affixed to medieval documents) or Long Term Validation (LTV). Because certificates can be revoked, it is important to keep a record of the certificate's validity *at the time of signing*. PDFs with LTV embed the result of a query—using what is known as the Online Certificate Status Protocol (OCSP)—that checks whether or not a certificate has been revoked.

Electronic signatures are now legal in most countries. Without digital signatures, the internet would cease to function. While these systems are constantly evolving (blockchain technology could eliminate PKI's dependence on certificate authorities, arguably the weakest link in digital security), they provide a safer signature than biometric identification, less prone to bias and abuse by the state.

7 PAW PRINTS & ICE CORES

Somewhere within Helsinki's Kiasma Museum of Contemporary Art, I am frozen, watching Marja Helander's short film *Birds in the Earth* (*Eatnanvuloš Lottit*), over and over, transfixed. It opens with two young women dressed in white tutus, toeing synchronized steps through the northern winter landscapes of Inari and Utsjoki. They are twins. Like Helander, the dancers, Birit and Katja Haarla, identify as Sámi, the historically nomadic peoples of Fennoscandia. They float across ice, empty towns, Arctic tundra, orange lichens, spongy turf.

Their routine is based on *The Dying Swan*, originally created by Mikhail Fokine for Anna Pavlova. Fokine's choreography was inspired by Tennyson's "The Dying Swan," part of a poetic series he termed "Animate Nature." In the poem, a wild swan's "death-hymn" echoes over a countryside that ripples with nonhuman life. A river runs with "inner voice," the wind sighs, a willow literally weeps, and a shepherd, the only human figure, becomes indistinct among "creeping mosses and clambering weeds."[1]

Birds in the Earth similarly blurs the boundary between humans, animals, and their geography. In one memorable shot—presumably made with a drone, but which feels like it is transmitted from the mind of a bird—interwoven tracks traverse an otherwise unmarked landscape of snow and trees. It is hard to tell if the marks are the tread signatures of dancers, reindeer, moose, a monstrous stylus, or something else.

I later read David Abram, who thinks that snow once served as proto paper. By tracing "the impression left by a deer's body in the snow, or transferring that outline onto the wall of the cave," he believes that ancient cultures collected "signatures not only of the human form but of other animals, trees, sun, moon, and landforms."[2]

The serious film erupts with unexpected humor. Suddenly the ballerinas find themselves in front of Helsinki's House of Parliament, dressed in Sámi costumes, blue *gátki* with red embroidery, traditionally worn while herding. And herding they are, in a way: a taxidermied reindeer joins them in the city. The animal is fixed in a state of confusion; so too are we.

Helander wanted to make a film that contrasted a disciplined artform with wild nature, to discuss the "contradiction between the Sámi people and the state of Finland." But she is hesitant to frame her work as political allegory. "My film is not a statement or a pamphlet," she says; "I think that in a work of art there should be something unexplainable."[3]

It's difficult to gauge whether whimsy is also irony. In a filmed interview, the director's spoken replies are imposed over footage of her whistling. She seems to be telling a joke that we do not know. When the interview ends, Helander's knees slowly bend, the old elevator trick, until she can no longer be seen by the static camera. She has sunken into the earth.

Doctrine of Signatures

We cannot think about the origins of signature without talking about the natural world. During the medieval and early-modern era, this correspondence became further systematized (and humanized) by *the doctrine of signatures*. While the *doctrine* concerned the signatures of plants and animals, it is thoroughly anthropocentric. "The general belief was that all things were made with reference to man," writes Edward Eggleston. "The wild woods were full of creatures whose value was written on each of them in the language of signatures, if the seeker for simples could only manage to decipher the label with which it had been considerably tagged at the creation."[4] Distinct from language, the *doctrine* posits that essences necessarily express themselves visibly—akin to Lombroso's idea that the handwriting of criminals could predict specific kinds of crime. Here again we find a version of *the law of similarity*. Think of the *doctrine of signatures* as a kind of divine user manual, which had a great influence on many areas of early-modern life.

The *doctrine* informed diets, governed the use of aphrodisiacs, and impacted medical treatment.[5] Euphrasia or eyebright, for example, was thought to possess a signature that aligned it with human eyes. As Paracelsus wrote: "Why does *Euphrasia* cure the eyes? Because it has in itself the *anatomiam oculorum*; it has in itself the shape and image of the eyes, and hence it becomes entirely eye."[6] To *become entirely eye* is different from representation; it implies that eyebright and the eye are connected through a divine system.

All things, animals, and people manifest their invisible qualities through visible signatures, for those who believe the *doctrine*. The trick comes in knowing where to look and how to interpret the world's hieroglyphs. Signatures "disclose unobserved proprieties not only in the vegetable shop, but the whole volume of nature," noted Thomas Browne.[7] This idea has all but died out, but we continue to invest our signatures with magical thinking.

Animal Tracks

As the filmmaker suggested on Syros, signatures are a kind of interscalar inscription—linking the genetic to the planetary. Watching Helander's film, I am reminded of Emerson's startling essay on Goethe, where he discusses the signature as a form of writing that resists anthropocentrism. "The air is full of sounds; the sky, of tokens; the round is all memoranda and signatures, and every object covered over with hints which speak to the intelligent."[8] While *the doctrine of signatures* involved plants and animals, it still relied upon the human eye to decipher the divine order of our world. Emerson does not prescribe an ideal reader. Animals and the earth write their own histories, in the form of tracks, furrows, striation. For whom?

The history of writing is full of fables. One needs repeating. According to Carlo Ginzburg, narrative—that most human of properties, the capacity to tell stories—was gleaned from the animal world. "Man has been a hunter for thousands of years. In the course of countless chases he learned to reconstruct the shapes and movements of his invisible prey from tracks on the ground, broken branches, excrement, tufts of hair, entangled feathers, stagnating odors."[9] Here we have the same claim as the *doctrine*, that language once dwelled within the animal world, but drained of its humanism. By tracking animal "prints," we learned to *read* signatures, to reconstruct an unseen animal from the traces it leaves behind. (Johanna Drucker recounts a parallel myth from India, where Ganesh, the elephant God, "broke off a tusk and used it as a pen.")[10]

Ginzburg admits that his thesis is obviously indemonstrable, but if we follow this thought experiment to its conclusion, what limits "printing" to the biological? Think about the geologic record: scientists are able to reconstruct the history of the earth's tectonic movements from lines left in stone, readable with the right techniques.

Carl Sagan makes a curious point in this regard. He thinks that animal prints share features with the surfaces of distant planets. His 1994 "lost lecture" has a curious history of its own: believed by his wife, the writer-producer Ann Druyan, to be Sagan's finest talk, the recording was misplaced for many years and only recently discovered on a dusty Sony Betacam tape.

In the lecture, Sagan discusses the indigenous San of the Kalahari Desert, as if walking abreast their hunt. "They take one close look at the ground. Immediately they know: how many animals went by; what their ages and sexes were; how long ago they passed," he says. He thinks that tracks work like signatures and that the San are graphologists of the hoofprint.

> But the decay of the hoof crater, the falling of pebbles in, the collapse of the raised rims, debris blown into it, tells you age, and, in fact, it reminds me of nothing so much as determining ages of planetary surfaces by looking at how fresh the impact craters are. I think the reason studying cratering physics seems so natural to us is because we have been doing it for a million years.[11]

It's a breathtaking image: an animal-print-become-celestial-crater, seductive for anyone who has gazed at rock paintings. Our most idealistic scientific project, searching for the signatures of life on other planets—the dream that has launched a thousand rocket ships—is simultaneously a quest inward and backward, toward the birth of our species on earth. It is also a sloppy equation of the indigenous and the prehistorical. Sagan acts as if the San are frozen in a certain period of world-historical development.

In this final chapter, I examine two kinds of more-than-human markings: epigenetic signatures and the climate signatures retrieved from ice cores. Like zooming out from a pebble to planet, signatures can be found on both the terrestrial and celestial scales, the microscopic and galactic. This is, of course, partially a play of the human mind. "We have, in other words, lived in a universe made sensible through patterns repeated on every scale, defined by the words we use to name it and the stories and metaphors we use to explain it and that come to substitute it," writes Judith Roof.[12]

Epigenetic Signatures

It will not surprise you—given the history of biometric signatures—that "DNA fingerprinting" is a contentious form of forensic identification.[13] Criminological analysis tempts researchers not just to match *like with like*, but to try and reconstruct phenotype from genotype, to deduce a person's bodily features from their genetic profile. Forensic technicians have traditionally used "extragenic" regions of DNA for evidence; that is, sequences that are not expressed as "detectable, physical traits."[14]

Experts worry that future efforts, some already underway, to produce "genetic mugshots" may fall prey to the same kind of manipulation associated with fingerprinting and physiognomy in the nineteenth century—using genetic data for profiling rather than identification. "Technologies promising to provide reliable knowledge of individual human subjects are the constant companions of efforts to control personal and collective action in all societies."[15] And technologies for creating and retrieving signatures, as we have seen, are often exploited by disciplinary agents to regulate populations.

The fast-growing field of epigenetics offers a different way of thinking about the communicative possibilities of signatures on a biological scale. It's important to recognize that language allows us to access certain ideas in layman's terms, but also frames and alters the object itself. Genetic research has long been discussed using textual metaphors. Sequences of nucleic acids are "read"; nucleotides are "letters"; the "information" in DNA is "copied" and extracted through "transcription" and "translation."[16]

The gene has held a totemic position in popular science since DNA came on the scene. In recent years, however, researchers have been excited by the "epigenome"—the chemical compounds affixed to DNA that are not part of the molecule itself. The theory has been around for a while (Conrad Waddington was writing about epigenetic landscapes in the 1940s, before scientists discovered the structure of DNA).[17] These epigenetic additions can regulate how genes are expressed. We might think of DNA as a signature's alphabetic letters and epigenetic features as the script that personalizes the characters: a collection of serifs, curls, and accents.

The epigenetic "revolution" has captured the public imagination for many reasons, but the most tangible draw concerns the perennial question of nature versus nurture.[18] Environmental influences show up in the epigenome; diet and exposure to pollution, for example, are thought to affect genetic expression.[19] And some believe that these changes can be passed to offspring, resurrecting a kind of Lamarckism for the twenty-first century: a tattoo transferred from parent to child.[20] While Darwinian evolution provides a theory for understanding genetic shifts, epigenetics may demonstrate a complementary pathway of inheritance, one in which the gene itself remains unmodified (critics are quick to point out that the methyl groups appended to DNA—one type of environmental signature—are rarely inherited beyond a few generations, however).[21] Epigenetics has led to a proliferation of science fiction, not yet substantiated.[22]

These misunderstandings trickle up. A *New Yorker* article on the subject by the esteemed Siddhartha Mukherjee was met with outcry in 2016.[23] The problem stemmed from metaphors. Nobel Laureate Sidney Altman commented: "I am not aware that there is such a thing as an epigenetic code," referring to Mukherjee's description of how biochemist Danny Reinberg's research sought "a whole animal, not just a cell, whose form and identity could be shifted by shifting the epigenetic code"; while Steven Henikoff from the Fred Hutchinson Cancer Research Center wrote—"He made it seem as if a healed broken ankle, and even a mere callus, become 'etched' into the genome."[24] *Coding* and *etching*, but what about signatures?

The epigenetic *signature* has not yet received the same critical attention as a textual metaphor from historians of science interested in rhetoric, yet it is ubiquitous across journals of repute. Some scientists search for epigenetic signatures of aging, attempting to locate a mechanism for determining biological youth in contrast to chronological age, while others seek biomarkers that indicate that an individual has been exposed to tobacco smoke.

Epigenetic signatures look nothing alike—the term has been used for describing both DNA methylation and histone modifications, for example—but refer to any changes that recur in the presence of a certain variable. There are millions of potential epigenetic signatures, but all involve parallel forms of repetition and recognition to those we find in autography. Either different bodies respond similarly to a common environmental factor, or heterogenous events—varying kinds of stress, for example—modify the epigenome in homologous ways.

Signatures play between duplication and difference, the personal and communal. And they remind us of the biological processes common across lifeforms (mouse models are a common human surrogate). For the first time in history, thanks to ongoing advancements, epigenetic signatures are becoming visible, telling complex stories about the traces life leaves upon a body, the way a biological entity becomes inscribed by its environment. We are never walled off from the world: at a microscopic scale, we are indistinct from it.

Ice Cores

A quick story. It's 355 and the Roman general Claudius Silvanus is unhappy with his lot in Gaul. People gossiped then as they do now. By the time word of his discontent reaches the Emperor Constantius II, it has been transformed—by telephone game—into high treason. The rumor is substantiated by a forgery. Procuring letters of recommendation from Silvanus, a dexterous informer "effaced the lines of writing, leaving only the signature intact, and wrote above it another text far different from the original."[25]

The forgery came to light, but, making fiction into fact, Silvanus responded with escalation. His troops declared him Emperor; twenty-eight days later, other soldiers took action, assassinating the usurping general. Some modern scholars believe that the tale is itself a fake, invented by Ammianus Marcellinus, whose *History* recounts the demise. Their proof? It seems that Silvanus never minted coins bearing his name and physiognomy: the standard technique for usurpers to gain authority and seize imperial power.[26]

Now let's widen the frame, from an individual to an empire. I tell you this story because it forms part of a larger narrative, signatures of which we can read on a geologic scale. Silvanus lived in the wake of what is known as *the crisis of the third century*. After the assassination of Severus Alexander the Roman Empire faced a power vacuum, exasperated by numerous, destabilizing geopolitical factors. This unrest led to the further debasement of the silver *denarius*—which, for centuries, had circulated as a standard unit of currency in Rome.

Silver production flourished in times of peace and stalled in war. The *denarius* was diluted during the third century's upheaval (some argue that Roman emperors stretched the metal to pay for their power struggles).[27] Silvanus's forged signature and his lack of currency bookend a longer trend, the record of which can now be read in the most unlikely of places: deep within northern ice.

Zoom out again, from an empire to an ice sheet: almost two miles thick in some places and astoundingly ancient at its deepest points. To study climate history, scientists drill what are called *ice cores*: a type of paleothermometer—like tree rings, ocean sediment, and fossil pollen—that grants access to earth's climate history. (In 2017, an ice core in Antarctica contained a sample thought to be 2.7 million years old.) As snow falls and freezes, it traps air and impurities in "readable" layers. The ice core is a vertical timeline; the past equals depth.

An example of a captured impurity? Lead. In 2018, a team of climate scientists, historians, and archaeologists published a paper arguing that atmospheric lead measurements, detected in ice cored from Greenland, track the political stability and economic history of Rome.[28] During times of economic health, silver mining accelerated, and pollution surged (large quantities of lead are released into the air during smelting). When the *denarius* was debased, mining slowed and lead levels fell. The nadir of atmospheric measurements during the Roman Empire? The crisis of the third century.

Climatologists call the data collected from ice cores *climate signatures*. These gases and debris are geological time machines, memories encoded in the planet's surface, retrievable with the right techniques. While conversations related to the Anthropocene—the geological period in which humans become a geophysical force—have only emerged in recent decades, the earth has been listening for much longer.

"What signatures our species will leave in the strata!" exclaims Robert Macfarlane in *Underland*, his study of deep time and subterranean landscapes.[29] The signatures on his mind are ugly things: flotillas of plastic in the Pacific Ocean. But ice cores are beautiful objects—devastation only becomes visible on a different scale.

Artist Peggy Weil has been thinking about one core in particular: what is known as GISP2D, extracted from the Greenland Summit. It contains "perhaps the most distinct layering of all the cores collected so far."[30] Weil's project, *88 Cores*, includes a video installation: working with eighty-eight sections of GISP2D, she scanned the ice and stitched its images together. This is bone-numbing work. The cores are kept in a freezer at minus thirty-eight degrees Fahrenheit (about where the scale converges with Celsius). Each sample must sit for six to eight hours before scanning can commence, in a room that is just a few degrees warmer.

Her project began as a search for visible signatures of climate events. During our correspondence, Weil recalls gasping while opening a canister known as 2465 (named after its depth in meters), containing a section dated

FIGURE 10

somewhere between 51,000 and 52,000 BCE. In the midst of this core, there is a thick black bar, which makes the ice look like a retracted document—censored by ash from a volcanic eruption in the distant past.

"Ice cores are now almost universally considered to be the best evidence of climate change," writes Carolyn Kormann, and Weil "unburies these ghostly hieroglyphs . . . reminding us that time is running out to decipher their meaning."[31] When I ask Weil about signatures, she points me toward a quotation from Swiss glaciologist Henri Bader: "Snowflakes fall to earth and leave a message."

The greatest irony in the history of signature is that a few serpentine lines might have curbed all of this—and can still. "The world's major powers came within several signatures of endorsing a binding, global framework to reduce carbon emissions—far closer than we've come since," writes Nathaniel Rich in a controversial exposé, referring to a decade between the late 1970s and 1980s.[32] A shape like the snake that proceeded our Fall could secure a future with the right new deal.

* * *

The end of a book is not the place to trot out watchwords and warhorses, but I cannot separate the climate crisis from the ego's deceptions, our unwavering attachment to a signature, the way it tricks us into isolation. "We are full to the gorge with our own names for misery," writes Djuna Barnes. "We are but skin about a wind, with muscles clenched against mortality.

We sleep in long reproachful dust against ourselves."[33] In her novel *Nightwood*, the vital and inert are two movements of one extended symphony: crest and trough of a continuous wave.

Life does not perch on the planet's indifferent surface—it is its manifestation. "We are the land," writes Paula Gunn Allen, but we treat the earth as "an ever-dead other that supplies us with a sense of ego identity by virtue of our contrast to its perceived non-being."[34] The spinal shiver of aesthetic experience; an earthquake's seismic ripples; a shaking dog, shedding water; the pen spidering above a dotted line . . . emanations of a singular system.

Similar arguments have been used to dodge responsibility. *If we are the earth, what we're doing is natural.* That's not what I'm peddling. But I also don't think we should strive to be Adam, steward of the garden, naming animals into dominion, nor Noah, bioengineering his cruise ship for all tomorrow's orgies. These are the ideas that first tipped the scale; a version of *saving the earth* simply means saving ourselves, or marketing Capitalism Lite®, without confronting why, for thousands of years, civilizations have felt alienated from the ground beneath their feet, the animals that walk upon it. The history of handwritten signatures—of the individual leaving his mark, extending a self, desperate for recognition—wraps around these questions.

We sleep in dust against ourselves . . . but what if we awoke? Researching ice cores, I learn of Julie Cruikshank's conversations with First Nations women in Yukon Territory. "They spoke about glaciers familiarly and often by name, well aware of their dangers, and they integrated accounts of glacier behaviour into narratives of their own experience. [They] portrayed glaciers as conscious and responsive to humans."[35] Were they wrong?

Science is now learning to read the signatures in ice, the way it reacts to global activity, but other paradigms have been seeing them longer. Many refuse to recognize this chiasmic enfolding of humans and nonhumans because it calls into question our narratives of dominance and destiny. "We were created that the earth might be made sensible of her inhuman taste," writes Barnes.[36]

Secular humanism smuggles in theistic ideas about life and death. Yet it fails to provide religion's calmatives, beyond an awkward back pat, specious stuff about having played some small—but not insignificant!—part in progress. Parents can find hope in knowing that their genetic code will survive them. In an unknown future, a child's face might flicker with your physical signature, a phenotypic likeness. But otherwise, modern death is quarantined from our culture. No wonder the rich and dying fancy themselves cryonic Pharaohs.

But peace enters in, the mystics say, once we relinquish the names and signatures to which we cling. Is there another sense of an ending, a *going gentle* when it's time? Lao Tzu teaches that naming is the origin of "all particular things"; on the scale of deep time, where the ice cores dwell, "the particular is always rendered anonymous," writes Jeffrey Jerome Cohen.[37] If we could come to terms with individual finitude, accept the coming catastrophe of our own personalities, would we begin to rid the earth from this cascading death, collectively wrought?

Of course, these are not the policy interventions immediately required. But what percentage of our greenhouse gas expenditure comes from trying to make a name? From carving out a legacy? Signatures writ large and small, extending a self across the world. Is there another way? One that would not urge us to scratch window panes, collect autographs, tattoo unwilling skin, or sign names onto Chartres, just to affirm our own particularity?

After burial, a corpse quickly decomposes. Its genetic data, fingernails, and vital organs are broken down by enzymes, bacteria, worms. Simplified elements become nutrition for plants, which nourish larger beings: *dust to dust*, but then life once more. Some of us will join subducting plates, plunging into the earth's mantle, and emerge as gems, garnet and beryl. Others will become part of the sea, where limestone forms, the kind that makes cliffs and cave walls, the kind that preserves the scratch marks of bears and humans, or creatures yet to come.

Though our bodies recombine completely, we can live on, for a time, through our signatures: fragments of DNA, handprints, writing, and neuronal impressions, burned into the minds of loved ones. We endure after our passing, but we will never be whole again. I'm starting to think this is a beautiful vision of eternity. To be one for a while, then many forever. *Who need be afraid of the merge?*

EPILOGUE

"I will come back for you!" promised Nikos, our ferryman, as we jumped from his yellow cruiser into the sea. He had anchored in a cove with fixed palm umbrellas, startling the goats sleeping beneath. While their bells sounded up through the hills that ran down to the shore, we hiked the coast to a distant peninsula.

If there was more time, I would tell you about the inscriptions we found: worn alphabets and young arabesques, the latter etched with penknives. They look like graffiti and feel like religion. The rock itself seems important, soft enough to receive autographs, harder than the erosive force of a thousand years of waves. The oldest writings are signed by pagan cults, Jewish travelers, and Christians during the Byzantine era. This little cove saw sailors from Thrace, the Dardanelles, Syria, Cilicia, Egypt, and further abroad. For now, though, you will have to imagine the prayers and the names and the vanished hands.

Before leaving Greece, I drive to meet Teos Romvos—poet, filmmaker, and ecological activist—in Ano Syros. I am drawn to Teos because of his unique book *Traces* (*IXNH*), which records every inscription that he has encountered on the island; and to Ano Syros because of Herman Melville's memorable description of the mountain town.[1] "The houses seemed clinging round its top, as if desperate for security, like shipwrecked men about a rock beaten by billows."[2] There is nothing desperate about this late summer evening, however, when Teos meets me by the pharmacy and we climb a hundred stairs to his home: the color of amaranth, with lime shutters.

I grow aware of my impoverished tongue. Twirling a white beard that kisses the collar of his patterned silk button-up, Teos says that he speaks French, Greek, and German fluently, and, for our conversation, can make do in English. I also meet Chara Pelekanou (an archaeologist, his partner) who sparked Teos's interest in inscriptions. We do not share a language, but I watch her roll out dough for *marathopites*— pie from fennel, gathered fresh. The kitchen is full of other smells that I cannot name. Later, Chara will kindly feed me, and I will feel like one of the dozen cats that pass through the house during our evening together.

"I like the traces," Teos says. "That, for me, is the motivation. The traces we leave behind us. That's the reason I searched not only for the old inscriptions, but also graffiti, because it is the same thing."

On the terrace, Teos points across the pink water, toward the island of Delos, "where Apollo was born." We begin to talk of plants and animals, the signatures they leave on Syros. He has been making films about how the island is changing.

As the light fades, Teos tells me about a species of fish that emerge from the sea to mate in the night. Although he has never seen them, he has seen the traces they leave in sand.

Yet when I play back the interview tape, months later, with snow falling fast outside my window in Finland, I cannot find the story, no matter how many times I listen. It has washed away.

ACKNOWLEDGMENTS

It would be impossible to write a book about signatures without cosigners. My gratitude to the Master and Fellows of Peterhouse for their support and collegiality. I have benefited from generous interlocutors—many appear by name in the text and notes. A few do not: Benjamin Abrams, Dane Brodke, Daisy Dixon, Uliana Dobrova, Abbie Garrington, Ben Goldstein, Amir Hay, Sarah Hopkinson, Dylan Howell, Laura Kilbride, Ewan Marsden, Paul McMullen, Jacob Moe, Nicholas Mulder, Donald Okpalugo, Sophie Pinkham, Cal Revely-Calder, Mikey Segel, Jo Rad Silver, Noah Sneider, McNeil Taylor, Jennifer Wallace, Sasha Winkler, and Nathaniel Zetter. Arden Reed did not get to read this book but showed me how to write it. *Kiitos* to my Finnish family (Nanna, Mika, Essi, Joonas, Minna, Tapio, Pip, Peter, Edvin). And to Emma, for everything . . .

NOTES

Chapter 1

1 Stacey Cowley, "No More Hasty Scrawls: The End of Credit Card Signatures," *New York Times* (April 9, 2018): B1.

2 Mario Carpo, *The Alphabet and the Algorithm* (Cambridge, MA: MIT Press, 2011), 3.

3 Sonja Neef, *Imprint and Trace: Handwriting in the Age of Technology*, trans. Anthony Matthews (London: Reaktion, 2011), 46.

4 Dylan Thomas, *Selected Poems: 1934–1952* (New York: New Directions, 2003), 67.

5 David Wills, *Inanimation: Theories of Inorganic Life* (Minneapolis: University of Minnesota Press, 2016), 46.

6 Josh Lauer, "Traces of the Real: Autographomania and the Cult of Signers in Nineteenth-Century America," *Text and Performance Quarterly* 27.2 (April 2007): 144.

7 Charles Lamb, *The Essays of Elia and The Last Essays of Elia* (Oxford: Oxford University Press, 1919), 15.

8 Vilém Flusser, *Does Writing Have a Future?*, trans. Nancy Ann Roth (Minneapolis: University of Minnesota Press, 2011), 17–22.

9 Anna Munster, *Materializing New Media: Embodiment in Information Aesthetics* (Hanover, NH: Dartmouth College Press, 2006), 21.

10 Lauer, "Traces of the Real," 147.

11 Elizabeth A. Meyer, *Legitimacy and Law in the Roman World: Tabulae in Roman Belief and Practice* (Cambridge: Cambridge University Press, 2004), 180.

12 James A. Harris, *Hume: An Intellectual Biography* (Cambridge: Cambridge University Press, 2015), 549.n48.

13 Virginia Woolf, *The Waves* (New York: Harcourt, 2005), 121.

14 J. L. Austin, *How to Do Things with Words* (Oxford: Clarendon Press, 1962), 61.

15 Bernard Siegert, *Cultural Techniques: Grids, Filters, Doors, and Other Articulations of the Real*, trans. Geoffrey Winthrop-Young (New York: Fordham University Press, 2015), 94.

16 Jeffrey M. Hurwit, *Artists and Signatures in Ancient Greece* (Cambridge: Cambridge University Press, 2015), 82.

17 Douglas Kahn, *Noise, Water, Meat: A History of Sound in the Arts* (Cambridge, MA: M.I.T. Press, 1999), 8.

18 Anne Trubek, *The History and Uncertain Future of Handwriting* (London: Bloomsbury, 2016), 71–82.

19 Rosemary Sassoon, *Handwriting of the Twentieth Century* (London: Routledge, 1999), 40; see also Béatrice Fraenkel, *La Signature, genèse d'un signe* (Paris: Gallimard, 1992).

20 Rudyard Kipling, "On Signatures," *The Cause of Humanity and Other Stories* (Cambridge: Cambridge University Press, 2018), 156.

Chapter 2

1 In writing on a film about forgery that is itself a fake, I have taken certain liberties.

2 Cecil Headlam, *The Story of Chartres* (London: J.M. Dent, 1902), 120.

3 Gilbert Millstein, *New York: True North* (New York: Doubleday, 1964), 45.

4 Joris-Karl Huysmans, *The Cathedral*, trans. Clara Bell (New York: New Amsterdam, 1898), 181.

5 Dorothy Molloy, *Hare Soup* (London: Faber & Faber, 2004), 32–3.

6 Jonathan Rosenbaum, *Discovering Orson Welles* (Berkeley: University of California Press, 2007), 56.

7 All Elmyr stories are gleaned from Clifford Irving, *Fake!: The Story of Elmyr de Hory, the Greatest Art Forger of Our Time* (New York: McGraw-Hill, 1969) and Mark Forgy, *The Forger's Apprentice: Life with the World's Most Notorious Artist* (Scotts Valley, CA: CreateSpace, 2012). Given that Irving was subsequently imprisoned for writing a fake autobiography of Howard Hughes, many accounts are, undoubtedly, fake.

8 Carlo Ginzburg, *Clues, Myths, and the Historical Method*, trans. John and Anne C. Tedeschi (Baltimore: Johns Hopkins University Press, 1989), 100.

9 Rosenbaum, *Discovering Orson Welles*, 290.

10 Sally Price, *Primitive Art in Civilized Places* (Chicago: University of Chicago Press, 2001), 100–7. See also: Jennifer C. Lena, *Entitled: Discriminating Tastes and the Expansion of the Arts* (Princeton, NJ: Princeton University Press, 2019), 93.

11 For an account of dissent, see Livio Pestilli, "The Artist's Signature as a Sign of Inauthenticity," *Source* 32.3 (Spring 2013): 5–16.

12 Kenneth Dauber, "The Indian Arts Fund and the Patronage of Native American Arts," in *Paying the Piper: Causes and Consequences of Art Patronage*, ed. Judith H. Balfe (Urbana: University of Illinois Press, 1993), 89.

13 Max Horberry, "The Artist Beneath the Art Forger," *New York Times* (February 22, 2020): C1.

14 Jonathan Lethem, *The Ecstasy of Influence: Nonfictions, etc.* (London: Jonathan Cape, 2012), 105.

15 For a discussion of this question, see the preface in John Wilmerding's *Signs of the Artist: Signatures and Self-Expression in American Paintings* (New Haven, CT: Yale University Press, 2003).

16 MishMash, "A Brief History of Art by Your Own Hands," http://www.mishmash.ru/Venus.html.

17 Lucian, *Affairs of the Heart*, trans. M. D. Macleod (Cambridge, MA: Harvard University Press, 1967), 173–7.

Chapter 3

1 Giorgio Agamben, *Nudities*, trans. David Kishlik and Stefan Pedatella (Palo Alto, CA: Stanford University Press, 2011), 38.

2 Zadie Smith, *On Beauty* (London: Penguin, 2005), 292.

3 Gerard Curtis, "Shared Lines: Pen and Pencil as Trace," *Victorian Literature and the Victorian Visual Imagination*, eds. Carol T. Christ and John O. Jordan (Berkeley: University of California Press, 1995), 32.

4 Michael North, *Camera Works: Photography and the Twentieth-Century Word* (Oxford: Oxford University Press, 2005), 4; Neef, *Imprint and Trace*, 32.

5 Walter Crane, *Line & Form* (London: G. Bell & Sons, 1900), 23. On Crane and visual signatures, see Johanna Drucker, *Visual Forms of Knowledge Production* (Cambridge, MA: Harvard University Press, 2014), 32–3.

6 Robert Macfarlane, *The Old Ways: A Journey on Foot* (London: Penguin, 2013), 52.

7 William Hogarth, *The Analysis of Beauty* (London: J. Reeves, 1753), xviii.

8 Samantha Matthews, "Psychological Crystal Palace? Late Victorian Confession Albums," *Book History* 3 (2000): 125.

9 Ibid., 126.

10 Ibid., 127.

11 Philip Roth, *My Life as a Man* (New York: Vintage, 2005), 4.

12 Joseph Conrad, *Typhoon & Other Tales* (London: The Folio Society, 2000), 27.

13 Annie Oppenheim, *Physiognomy Made Easy: Character as Expressed in the Human Countenance* (London: E. Cruse, c.1880), 3.

14 George Scarr Hall, *A Manual of Phrenology and Physiognomy, or, the Science of Reading Character by the Head and Face Made Easy* (Manchester: Brook and Chrystal, 1887), 8.

15 Rebecca West, *The Birds Fall Down* (New York: Open Road, 2010), Kindle edition, 187.

16 Alberto Manguel, "You Are How You Write: When Script Expresses Identity," *Times Literary Supplement* (March 12, 2019): https://www.the-tls.co.uk/articles/you-are-how-you-write/.

17 Walter Benjamin, "On the Mimetic Faculty," *Selected Writings*, trans. Rodney Livingstone et al., vol. 2.2 (Cambridge, MA: Harvard University Press, 1999), 491.

18 John Irwin, *American Hieroglyphics: The Symbol of the Egyptian Hieroglyphics in the American Renaissance* (Baltimore, MD: John Hopkins University Press, 2016), 44.

19 John Rexford, *What Handwriting Indicates: An Analytical Graphology* (New York: G. P. Putnam's Sons, 1904), 85.

20 Tamara Thornton, *Handwriting in America: A Cultural History* (New Haven, CT: Yale University Press, 1996), 84.

21 Barack Obama, *Public Papers of the President of the United States* (Washington, DC: United States Government Publishing Office, 2018), 11.

22 Michael Crowley, "Trump and Sharpie's Maker Land in Different Kind of Storm," *New York Times* (September 5, 2019): https://www.nytimes.com/2019/09/05/us/politics/trump-sharpie.html.

23 Hannah Knowles and Colby Itkowitz, "Nancy Pelosi gave out souvenir pens after sending impeachment to the Senate—and Republicans are fuming," *Washington Post* (January 16, 2020): https://www.washingtonpost.com/politics/2020/01/16/nancy-pelosi-pens-impeachment/.

24 Lily Pickard, "What Donald Trump's signature says about his personality, according to an expert," *Independent* (November 13, 2016): https://www.independent.co.uk/news/world/americas/us-elections/handwriting-signature-trump-us-election-analysis-what-does-it-say-expert-a7412131.html.

25 Claire Voon, "Trump's Signature is the 'Soundwave of Demons Screaming,'" *Hyperallergic* (January 30, 2017): https://hyperallergic.com/354588/trumps-signature-is-the-sound-wave-of-demons-screaming/.

26 Cesare Lombroso, *Criminal Man*, trans. Mary Gibson and Nicole Hahn Rafter (Durham, NC: Duke University Press, 2006), 55.

27 Ibid., 113.

28 Simon A. Cole, *Suspect Identities: A History of Fingerprinting and Criminal Identification* (Cambridge, MA: Harvard University Press, 2002), 58.

29 Autograph collecting might have first flourished alongside the invention of the printing press. See Lauer, "Autographomania," 147–8.

30 Thomas Hood, "An Autograph from Thomas Hood," *New Sporting Magazine* 19 (July 1840): 49.

31 Harry Furniss, "The Autograph Hunter," *Strand Magazine* 24 (November 1902): 542.

32 George J. Beesley, "My Shakespeare Autograph Book," *Strand Magazine* 25 (March 1903): 291.

33 Thomas Bailey Aldrich, *Ponkapog Papers* (Boston: Houghton, Mifflin & Co., 1903), 148.

34 Adrian Hoffman Joline, *Edgehill Essays* (Boston: The Gorham Press, 1911), 31.

35 Adrian Hoffman Joline, *Meditations of an Autograph Collector* (New York: Harper & Brothers, 1902), 2.

36 Henry James, *The Notebooks of Henry James* (Oxford: Oxford University Press, 1947), 148–9.

37 Theodore F. Dwight, "Autographomania," *Overland Monthly* 3 (October 1869): 342.

38 Trubek, *Handwriting*, 100.

39 James Baldwin, "Sweet Lorraine," *Esquire* (November 1, 1969): 139.

40 Walter Benjamin, "Unpacking my Library," *Selected Writings, Vol 2: Part 2, 1931–1934* (Cambridge, MA: Belknap Press, 2005), 491. Italics mine.

41 Chris Gosden and Chantal Knowles, *Collecting Colonialism: Material Culture and Colonial Change* (Oxford: Berg, 2001), xix.

42 Cole, *Suspect Identities*, 54. Samuel J. Redman, *Bone Rooms: From Scientific Racism to Human Prehistory in Museums* (Cambridge, MA: Harvard University Press, 2016), 24.

43 Scott Richard Lyons, *X-Marks: Native Signatures of Assent* (Minneapolis: University of Minnesota Press, 2010), 1–2.

44 Alexandra Harmon, ed., *Rethinking Indian Treaties in the Pacific Northwest* (Seattle: University of Washington Press, 2008), 19.

45 Lauer, "Autographomania," 152.

46 Richard Ellmann, *Oscar Wilde* (London: Hamish Hamilton, 1987), 159.

47 Geoffrey Batchen, *Forget Me Not: Photography & Remembrance* (New York: Princeton Architectural Press, 2004), 65.

Chapter 4

1 Walter Benjamin, *The Arcades Project*, trans. Howard Eiland and Kevin McLaughlin (Cambridge, MA: Harvard University Press 1999), 9.

2 Andrew Barnett, *Sibelius* (New Haven, CT: Yale University Press, 2007), 191.

3 Antti Lahelma, *A Touch of Red: Archaeological and Ethnographic Approaches to Interpreting Finnish Rock Paintings* (Helsinki: The Finnish Antiquarian Society, 2008), 28–9.

4 Robert Layton, *Sibelius* (London: J.M. Dent and Sons, 1965), 16.

5 Burnett James, *The Music of Jean Sibelius* (Rutherford, NJ: Fairleigh Dickinson University Press, 1983), 70.

6 D. L. Hoffmann et al., "U-Th dating of carbonate crusts reveals Neandertal origin of Iberian cave art," *Science* 359 (2018): 912–15.

7 G. W. F. Hegel, *System of Ethical Life and First Philosophy of Spirit*, trans. H. S. Harris and T. M. Knox (Albany: State University of New York Press, 1979), 221.

8 Ismo Luukkonen, "Digital Retouching of Rock Paintings," (2019): http://www.ismoluukkonen.net/kalliotaide/docum/docum.html.

9 Edward T. Hall, *Beyond Culture* (New York: Anchor Books, 1989), 29.

10 Alfred Gell, *Art and Agency: An Anthropological Theory* (Oxford: Clarendon Press, 1994), 104.

11 Claude Lévi-Strauss, *Tristes Tropiques*, trans. John Russell (New York: Criterion Books, 1961), 270.

12   Colin MacCabe, "Claude Lévi-Strauss: the Poet in the Laboratory," *New Statesman* (November 4, 2010): https://www.newstatesman.com/books/2010/11/levi-strauss-writing-thought.

13   Perry Anderson, "The Mythologian," *New Left Review* 71 (September–October 2011): 135–40.

14   C. G. Jung, *Psychological Types*, trans. H. B. Baynes, rev.by R. F. C. Hull (Princeton, NJ: Princeton University Press, 1976), 631.

15   Lucien Lévy-Bruhl, *Primitive Mentality*, trans. Lilian A. Clare (London: George Allen & Unwin, 1923), 173.

16   James George Frazer, *The Golden Bough: A Study in Magic and Religion* (London: Macmillan, 1959), 11, 12.

17   Ibid., 244.

18   Michael Taussig, *Mimesis and Alterity: A Particular History of the Senses* (New York: Routledge, 1993), 47–8.

19   Julia Jacobs, "Wrecker of Trump Star Reaches a Plea Deal," *New York Times* (November 10, 2018): C3.

20   Neef, *Imprint and Trace*, 43.

21   Sarah Minor, "Handling the Beast," *Conjunctions* 61 (Fall 2013): 22.

22   Nicolás Salazar Sutil, *Matter Transmission: Mediation in a Paleocyber Age* (London: Bloomsbury, 2018), 167.

23   Georges Bataille, *Theory of Religion*, trans. Robert Hurley (New York: Zone Books, 1989), 19; Oxana Timofeeva, "'The Only Real Outlaws': Animal Freedom in Bataille," *Georges Bataille and Contemporary Thought*, ed. Will Stronge (London: Bloomsbury, 2017), 164.

24   Thomas Macho, "Second-Order Animals: Cultural Techniques of Identity and Identification," *Theory, Culture & Society* 30.6 (2013): 32.

25   Neef, *Imprint and Trace*, 45.

26   Maurice Blanchot, *Friendship*, trans. Elizabeth Rottenberg (Palo Alto, CA: Stanford University Press, 1997), 2, 11.

27   Hans-Georg Bandi et al., *The Art of the Stone Age*, trans. Ann E. Keep and Dr. Phil (New York: Crown, 1961), 52.

28 Judith Thurman, "First Impressions," *New Yorker* (June 16, 2008): https://www.newyorker.com/magazine/2008/06/23/first-impressions.

29 Neef, *Imprint and Trace*, 45.

30 Michel Serres, *Malfeasance: Appropriation through Pollution?*, trans. Anne-Marie Feenberg-Dibon (Palo Alto, CA: Stanford University Press, 2011), 2–3.

31 Werner Herzog, *Conquest of the Useless: Reflections from the Making of* Fitzcarraldo (New York: Ecco, 2009), 250.

32 Minor, "Handling the Beast," 21.

33 For an account of these objections, see Steven Roger Fischer, *A History of Writing* (London: Reaktion, 2003), 26–7.

34 Barry B. Powell, *Theory and History of the Technology of Civilization* (Chichester, UK: Wiley, 2012), 67–8. Denise Schmandt-Besserat, *When Writing Met Art: From Symbol to Story* (Austin: University of Texas Press, 2007), 27–8.

35 Ibid., 31.

36 The seals I reproduce are discussed in Schmandt-Besserat, *When Writing*, 30–5, who, in turn, reproduced them from Arthur J. Tobler, *Excavations at Tepe Gawra* vol. 2 (Philadelphia: University of Pennsylvania Press, 1950).

37 Kipling, "On Signatures," 154.

38 Collin G. Calloway, *Pen and Ink Witchcraft: Treaties and Treaty Making in American Indian History* (New York: Oxford University Press, 2013), 46.

39 Jacques Derrida, *Of Grammatology*, trans. Gayatri Spivak (Baltimore, MD: Johns Hopkins University Press, 1998), 287.

40 For a discussion of this history, see James C. Scott, *Against the Grain: A Deep History of the Earliest States* (New Haven, CT: Yale University Press, 2013).

41 Elif Batuman, "The Sanctuary," *New Yorker* (December 11, 2011): https://www.newyorker.com/magazine/2011/12/19/the-sanctuary.

42 For a letter-by-letter account, see Lyn Davies, *A is for Ox: A Short History of the Alphabet* (London: Folio Society, 2006). Johanna Drucker provides a nuanced elaboration in *The Alphabetic Labyrinth: The Letters in History and Imagination* (London: Thames & Hudson, 1995).

43 Andrew Robins, "The Alpha Hypothesis: Did Lateralized Cattle–Human Interactions Change the Script for Western Culture?" *Animals* 9.9 (2019): 638.

Chapter 5

1 Page duBois, *Out of Athens: The New Ancient Greeks* (Cambridge, MA: Harvard University Press, 2010), 70.

2 Nancy E. van Deusen, *Global Indios: The Indigenous Struggle for Justice in Sixteenth-Century Spain* (Durham, NC: Duke University Press, 2015), 136.

3 James Baldwin, *Notes of a Native Son* (London: Bantam Press, 1955), 144.

4 An account of tattoo inheritance can be found in Aristotle, *History of Animals*, VII–X (Cambridge, MA: Harvard University Press, 1991), 455.

5 Benedict Carey, "Can We Really Inherit Trauma?" *New York Times* (December 10, 2018): https://www.nytimes.com/2018/12/10/health/mind-epigenetics-genes.html.

6 Hortense J. Spillers, "Mama's Baby, Papa's Maybe: An American Grammar Book," *Diacritics* 17.2 (Summer 1987): 67. In correspondence, however, Amanda Reid reminds me that Spillers is "resisting a trauma narrative in which brokenness (brokenness of flesh or subjecthood) passes from one generation to another, and focusing instead on the power and transference of a *racial story* about social subjecthood that needs a certain kind of black feminist hermeneutic to heal."

7 "Erasing Type: Hank Willis Thomas on What Advertisements Are Really Saying," *Time* (April 19, 2011): https://time.com/3776410/what-advertisements-dont-say/.

8 Simone Browne, *Dark Matters: On the Surveillance of Blackness* (Durham, NC: Duke University Press, 2015), 94.

9 Spencer Schaffner, *Writing as Punishment in Schools, Courts & Everyday Life* (Tuscaloosa: University of Alabama Press, 2019), 68.

10 Herodotus, *The Histories*, trans. Robin Waterfield (Oxford: Oxford University Press, 2008), 420.

11 Maria L. La Ganga, "Alleged attackers wrote on Audrie Pott's body, lawyer says," *Los Angeles Times* (April 15, 2013): https://www.latimes.com/local/lanow/la-xpm-2013-apr-15-la-me-ln-alleged-attackers-wrote-on-audrie-pott-20130415-story.html.

12 Maggie Nelson, *Women, The New York School, and Other True Abstractions* (Iowa City: University of Iowa Press, 2007), 185.

13 Lea VanderVelde, *Redemption Songs: Suing for Freedom before Dred Scott* (New York: Oxford University Press, 2014), 92.

14 Drake feat. Rick Ross, "Free Spirit," *Care Package*, OVO Sound, 2019.

15 Meek Mill feat. John Legend, Nas, and Rick Ross, "Maybach Curtains," *Dreams and Nightmares*, Warner Records, 2012.

16 50 Cent, "Hold On," *Animal Ambition: An Untamed Desire to Win*, G-Unit, 2014.

17 Krista Thompson, *Shine: The Visual Economy of Light in African Diasporic Aesthetic Practice* (Durham, NC: Duke University Press, 2015), 215–70.

18 Method Man, "Bring the Pain," *Tical*, Def Jam Records, 1994.

19 Lil' Kim, "Who's Number One," *The Notorious K.I.M.*, Atlantic Records, 2000; Afu-Ra, "Bring it Right," *Body of the Life Force*, Gee Street Records, 2000; M.O.P., "Stand Up," *Mash Out Posse*, Family First Productions, 2004.

20 Erik Nielson, "'Can't C Me': Surveillance and Rap Music," *Journal of Black Studies* 40.6 (July 2010): 1260.

21 Digital Underground feat. Big Pun and BINC, "The Mission," *Who Got the Gravy?*, Jake Records, 1998; G-Unit feat. Joe, "Wanna Get to Know You," *Beg for Mercy*, G-Unit and Interscope, 2003.

22 Nancy Princenthal, *Unspeakable Acts: Women, Art, and Sexual Violence in the 1970s* (London: Thames & Hudson, 2019), 224.

23 Ramie Targoff, *John Donne: Body and Soul* (Chicago: University of Chicago Press, 2008), 67–8.

24 Gang Starr feat. J. Cole, "Family and Loyalty," TTT/Gang Starr Enterprises, 2019.

25 The verse was posthumously used in "The Dream Shatterer," *Endangered Species,* Loud Records, 2001. The cipher can be found here: https://www.youtube.com/watch?v=usyyz3wmsLg.

26 van Deusen, *Global Indios*, 133.

27 Run the Jewels feat. Zach de la Rocha, "Close Your Eyes (And Count to Fuck)," *Run the Jewels 2*, Mass Appeal Records, 2014.

28 Friedrich Kittler, *Gramophone, Film, Typewriter*, trans. Geoffrey Winthrop-Young and Michael Wutz (Palo Alto, CA: Stanford University Press, 1999), 186–7.

29 Mario Codognato, *Piero Manzoni: Works 1957–1961* (London: Karsten Schubert, 1989), 9.

30 Maggie Nelson, *Bluets* (Seattle, WA: Wave Books, 2009), 49–50.

31 *The Pillow Book of Sei Shonagon*, trans. Ivan Morris (London: The Folio Society, 1979), 201.

32 My gratitude to Aaron Kunin, whose ideas are strewn across this book. He develops Donne's "topping from the bottom" in *Love Three: A Study of a Poem by George Herbert* (Seattle, WA: Wave Books, 2019).

33 *R v Wilson* (1996) 2 Cr App Rep 241 Court of Appeal (Lord Justice Russell, Mrs. Justice Bracewell and The Recorder of Newcastle (Judge Stroyan Q.C.)): February 23, 29, 1996. Thanks to Charlotte Proudman for this reference.

34 Jeremy Broome, "Skin Writing," *Strand Magazine* 14 (1897): 453.

35 Georges Didi-Huberman, "The Figurative Incarnation of the Sentence: Notes on the 'Autographic' Skin," *Journal* 47.5: 69.

36 Vicki Kirby, *Telling Flesh: The Substance of the Corporeal* (New York: Routledge, 1997), 62.

37 Siri Hustvedt, *What I Loved: A Novel* (London: Sceptre, 2003), 74–5.

38 Asti Hustvedt, *Medical Muses: Hysteria in Nineteenth-Century Paris* (London: Bloomsbury, 2011).

39 Frances Perraudin, "Surgeon admits marking his initials on the livers of two patients," *Guardian* (December 13, 2017): https://www. theguardian.com/uk-news/2017/dec/13/surgeon-admits-marking-his-initials-on-the-livers-of-two-patients.

40   Lindsay Merbaum, "Skin Deep: A Profile of San Francisco Tattoo Artist Idexa Stern," (October 13, 2015): https://medium.com/@Merbizzle/skin-deep-a-profile-of-san-francisco-tattoo-artist-idexa-stern-da68cc8c6123.

41   Alisa Damaso, "Mariel Bayona / Traditional Artist," (November 18, 2014): http://www.killercreatives.com/mariel-bayona-traditional-artist/.

Chapter 6

1   When the novel was published in 1893, fingerprinting had not yet become an accepted forensic technique. Mark Twain, *Pudd'nhead Wilson and Those Extraordinary Twins* (New York: Modern Library, 2002), 169.

2   For Jefferson and the polygraph, see Louis McAurely, *Print Technology in Scotland and America, 1740–1800* (Lewisburg, PA: Bucknell University Press, 2013), 44–5; and Silvio Bedini, *Thomas Jefferson and His Copying Machines* (Charlottesville: University Press of Virginia, 1984).

3   Steven Connor, "Modes of Manifold Writing" (September 13, 2014): http://stevenconnor.com/polygraph.html.

4   Richard R. John, *Network Nation: Inventing American Telecommunications* (Cambridge, MA: Harvard University Press, 2010), 285.

5   David E. Brown, "What's in a Name," *Cabinet* 5 (Winter 2001–2002): http://www.cabinetmagazine.org/issues/5/whatsinaname.php.

6   Heidi Harralson, *Developments in Handwriting and Signature Identification in the Digital Age* (London: Routledge, 2013), 46.

7   Charles Hamilton, *The Robot That Helped to Make a President* (New York, 1965), 4. See Richard Grusin, "Signature Content: Handwriting in an Age of Digital Remediation," *Sign Here! Handwriting in the Age of New Media*, eds. Sonja Neef, José van Dijck, and Eric Ketelaar (Amsterdam: Amsterdam University Press, 2006), 95–115.

8   Joe Nickell, *Detecting Forgery: Forensic Investigation of Documents* (Lexington: University of Kentucky Press, 1996), 78–94.

9   Bill McCallister, "Autopen: A Powerful Sign of the Times in Washington," *Los Angeles Times* (October 1, 1989): https://www.latimes.com/archives/la-xpm-1989-10-01-vw-1151-story.html.

10 Brian Resnick, "When a Robot Signs a Bill: A Brief History of the Autopen," *Atlantic* (January 3, 2013): https://www.theatlantic.com/politics/archive/2013/01/when-a-robot-signs-a-bill-a-brief-history-of-the-autopen/454803/.

11 Michael Shear, "Making Legislative History, With Nod from Obama and Stroke of an Autopen," *New York Times* (May 28, 2011): A13.

12 Hamilton, *Robot*, 18.

13 Ibid., xiv.

14 Ibid., 8.

15 Bernard Cooper, "Out on a Limb," *Los Angeles Magazines* (September 2001): 140.

16 https://www.guggenheim.org/artwork/33834.

17 Agnieszka Kurant interviewed by Sabine Russ, *BOMB* (March 18, 2015): https://bombmagazine.org/articles/agnieszka-kurant/.

18 Friedrich Kittler, *Discourse Networks 1800/1900*, trans. Michael Metteer with Chris Cullens (Palo Alto, CA: Stanford University Press, 1992), 215.

19 Kittler, *Gramophone, Film, Typewriter*, 226.

20 Arthur Conan Doyle, *The New Annotated Sherlock Holmes*, vol. 1 (New York: Norton, 2005), 94.

21 Fabian Monrose and Aviel D. Rubin, "Keystroke dynamics as a biometric for authentication," *Future Generation Computer Systems* 16.4 (2000): 351–9.

22 Charles Dickens, *Great Expectations* (London: Penguin, 2003), 3.

23 Philp Hensher, *The Missing Ink* (London: Macmillan, 2012), 34.

24 Walter Benjamin, "The Paris of the Second Empire in Baudelaire," *Selected Writings 4* (Cambridge, MA: Belknap Press, 2006), 27.

25 alanasunny, Instagram, April 17, 2019: https://www.instagram.com/p/BwVypVAH8Ed/; @hetchserg, Twitter, April 15, 2019: https://twitter.com/hetchserg/status/1117859980965818374;

@ferrero365, Twitter, April 15, 2019: https://twitter.com/ferrero365/
status/1117866783346700290; the final post was found in the
comments section of the following news article, although, in the
course of writing this book, it subsequently disappeared (I failed to
note its author's name at the time; lessons were learned about the
fragility of signatures): Maham Abedi and Jesse Ferreras, "Notre
Dame cathedral fire is under control, Paris firefighters say," *Global
News* (April 15, 2019): https://globalnews.ca/news/5168799/fire-tears-
through-notre-dame-cathedral-in-paris/.

26   Roland Barthes, *Camera Lucida: Reflections on Photography* (New
York: Hill and Wang, 1981), 97.

27   Susan Sontag, *On Photography* (New York: Farrar, Straus and Giroux,
1977), 70.

28   Lisa Gitelman, *Scripts, Grooves, and Writing Machines: Representing
Technology in the Edison Era* (Palo Alto, CA: Stanford University
Press, 2000), 3.

29   Bertrand Russell, *The Basic Writings of Bertrand Russell* (London:
Routledge, 2009), 82.

30   https://bigbrotherwatch.org.uk/2018/06/hmrc/.

31   Cole, *Suspect Identities*, 61.

32   Henry Faulds, *Dactylography: or, The Study of Finger Prints* (Halifax,
UK: Milner & Co., c.1912), 10–11.

33   Joseph Pugliese, *Biometrics: Bodies, Technologies, Biopolitics* (New
York: Routledge, 2010), 48–50.

34   Cole, *Suspect Identities*, 3.

35   Apple, "Face ID Security" (November 2017): https://www.apple.com/
business/docs/site/FaceID_Security_Guide.pdf.

36   Paul D. A. Harvey and A. McGuiness, *A Guide to British Medieval
Seals* (London: British Library, 1996), 2.

37   Charles Donahue, "History in Deed: Medieval Society & The Law
in England, 1100–1600" (October 13, 1993): https://hls.harvard.
edu/library/historical-special-collections/exhibits/history-in-deed-
medieval-society-the-law-in-england-1100-1600/#note16.

38   Macho, "Second-Order Animals," 41.

39   Stephen Mason, *Electronic Signatures in Law*, 3rd edition (Cambridge: Cambridge University Press, 2012), 60. I am indebted to Mason's excellent reference for many of the case histories in this chapter.

40   Ibid., 35.

41   Ibid., 341–2.

42   *In re Mayfield, 2016 WL 3958982, No. 16-22134-D-7 (E.D. Cal. July 15, 2016).*

43   For a collated list of objections, see Jennifer L. Mnookin, "Scripting Expertise: The History of Handwriting Identification Evidence and the Judicial Construction of Reliability," *Virginia Law Review* 87.8 (December 2001): 1723–1845; and Michael D. Risinger et al., "Exorcism of Ignorance as a Proxy for Rational Knowledge: The Lessons of Handwriting Identification 'Expertise,'" *University of Pennsylvania Law Review* 137 (1988–1989): 731–92.

44   Michael D. Risinger, "Goodbye to All That, or a Fool's Errand, By One of the Fools: How I Stopped Worrying about Court Responses to Handwriting Identification (and Forensic Science in General) and Learned to Love Misinterpretations of *Kumho Tire v. Carmichael*," *Tulsa Law Review* 43 (2013): 447–75.

45   Michael Kurland, *Irrefutable Evidence: Adventures in the History of Forensic Science* (Chicago: Ivan R. Dee, 2009), 61. Louis Menand, *The Metaphysical Club* (New York: Farrar, Straus and Giroux, 2002), 151–76.

Chapter 7

1   Alfred, Lord Tennyson, *Tennyson: A Selected Edition* (London: Routledge, 2007), 14–15.

2   David Abram, *The Spell of the Sensuous: Perception and Language in a More-Than-Human World* (New York: Vintage, 1996), 97.

3   Sundance Institute, "Short Competition: *Birds in the Earth*": https://www.youtube.com/watch?v=chpO7hE8oXU.

4 Edward Eggleston, *The Transit of Civilization: From England to America in the Seventeenth Century* (Boston: Beacon Hill, 1959), 69–70.

5 "Empty Signs? Reading the Book of Nature in Renaissance Science," *Studies in History and Philosophy of Science* 21.3 (1990): 512.

6 Giorgio Agamben, *The Signature of All Things: On Method*, trans. Luca D'Isanto and Kevin Attell (Cambridge, MA: MIT Press, 2009), 37.

7 Thomas Browne, *Hydriotaphia and the Garden of Cyrus* (London: Macmillan, 1896), 159.

8 Ralph Waldo Emerson, "Goethe; or, the Writer," *Essays & Lectures* (New York: Penguin Putnam, 1983), 716.

9 Ginzburg, *Clues*, 102.

10 Johanna Drucker, *Alphabetic Labyrinth: The Letters in History and Imagination* (London: Thames & Hudson, 1999), 22.

11 Thanks to Ryan Rafaty for this reference. Carl Sagan, "The Age of Exploration," Carl Sagan Institute: https://www.youtube.com/watch?v=6_-jtyhAVTc.

12 Judith Roof, *The Poetics of DNA* (Minneapolis: University of Minnesota Press, 2007), 25.

13 Naomi Elster, "How Forensic DNA Evidence Can Lead to Wrongful Convictions," *JSTOR Daily* (December 6, 2017): https://daily.jstor.org/forensic-dna-evidence-can-lead-wrongful-convictions/.

14 Michael Lynch et al., *Truth Machine: The Contentious History of DNA Fingerprinting* (Chicago: University of Chicago Press, 2008), 37.

15 Robin Williams, "DNA Databases and the Forensic Imaginary," *Genetic Suspects: Global Governance of Forensic DNA Profiling and Databasing*, eds. Richard Hindmach and Barbara Prainsack (Cambridge: Cambridge University Press, 2012), 131.

16 For a discussion of this, see Robert Pollack, *Signs of Life: The Language and Meanings of DNA* (Boston: Houghton Mifflin, 1995).

17 Erik L. Peterson, *The Life Organic: The Theoretical Biology Club and the Roots of Epigenetics* (Pittsburgh: University of Pittsburgh Press, 2016).

18   Nessa Carey, *The Epigenomic Revolution: How Modern Biology is Rewriting Our Understanding of Genetics, Disease and Inheritance* (New York: Columbia University Press, 2012).

19   Aaron D. Goldberg et al., "Epigenetics: A Landscape Takes Shape," *Cell* 128.4 (February 2007): 635–8.

20   Peter Ward, *How Epigenetics is Revolutionizing Our Understanding of Evolution's Past and Present* (New York: Bloomsbury, 2018).

21   Kevin Mitchell, "Grandma's trauma—a critical appraisal of the evidence for transgenerational epigenetic inheritance in humans," (May 29, 2018): http://www.wiringthebrain.com/2018/05/grandmas-trauma-critical-appraisal-of.html.

22   Steven Rose, "How to Get Another Thorax," *London Review of Books* 38.17 (September 8, 2016): 15–17.

23   Siddhartha Mukherjee, "Same but Different," *New Yorker* (April 25, 2016): https://www.newyorker.com/magazine/2016/05/02/breakthroughs-in-epigenetics.

24   Jerry Coyne, "The New Yorker screws up big time with science: researchers criticize the Mukherjee piece on epigenetics" (May 5, 2016): https://whyevolutionistrue.wordpress.com/2016/05/05/the-new-yorker-screws-up-big-time-with-science-researchers-criticize-the-mukherjee-piece-on-epigenetics/.

25   Ammianus Marcellinus, *History* (Cambridge, MA: Harvard University Press, 1950), 135.

26   Timothy D. Barnes, *Ammianus Marcellinus and the Representation of Historical Reality* (Ithaca, NY: Cornell University Press, 1998), 18–19.

27   Kevin Greene, *The Archaeology of the Roman Economy* (Berkeley: University of California Press, 1990), 61.

28   Joseph R. McConnell et al., "Lead pollution recorded in Greenland ice indicates European emissions tracked plagues, wars, and imperial expansion during antiquity," *Proceedings of the National Academy of Sciences* 115 (May 2018): 5726–5731; DOI:10.1073/pnas.1721818115.

29   Robert Macfarlane, *Underland* (London: Penguin, 2019), Kindle edition, 92.

30 Todd McLeish, *Narwhals: Artic Whales in a Melting World* (Seattle: University of Washington Press, 2013), 89.

31 Carolyn Kormann, "As the World Melts, an Artist Finds Beauty in Ancient Ice," *New Yorker* (February 9, 2018): https://www.newyorker.com/tech/annals-of-technology/as-the-world-melts-an-artist-finds-beauty-in-ancient-ice.

32 Nathaniel Rich, "Losing Earth: The Decade We Almost Stopped Climate Change," *New York Times* (August 1, 2018): https://www.nytimes.com/interactive/2018/08/01/magazine/climate-change-losing-earth.html.

33 Djuna Barnes, *Nightwood* (New York: New Directions, 2006), 90.

34 Paula Gunn Allen, *The Sacred Hoop: Recovering the Feminine in American Indian Traditions* (Boston: Beacon Press, 1983), 128.

35 Julie Cruikshank, *Do Glaciers Listen?: Local Knowledge, Colonial Encounters, and Social Imagination* (Vancouver: University of British Columbia Press, 2005), 8.

36 Barnes, *Nightwood*, 90.

37 *Tao Te Ching,* trans. Stephen Mitchell (New York: Harper Perennial, 1988), §1. Jeffrey Jerome Cohen, *Stone: An Ecology of the Inhuman* (Minneapolis: University of Minnesota Press, 2015), 72.

Epilogue

1 For an excerpt, see Teos Romvos, "Traces—The Stone Chronicle of Syros," trans. Rupert Smith (October 23, 2018): https://www.apanomeria.org/en/traces-the-stone-chronicle-the-island-syros/.

2 Herman Melville, *Journals* (Evanston, IL: Northwestern University Press, 1989), 71.

FIGURES

INDEX